I Believe

Fundamentals of the Christian Faith

Written by the Bible Faculty of
God's Bible School & College

I Believe
Fundamentals of the Christian Faith

Copyright 2006 Revivalist Press

First Printing January 2006
Second Printing August 2009

ISBN: 978-0-9749186-3-1

Publishing Ministry of

God's Bible School & College
1810 Young Street
Cincinnati, OH 45202
Revivalist@gbs.edu

All rights reserved. This book may not be reproduced in whole or in part without written permission from the publisher.

Printed by Country Pines, Inc., Shoals, Indiana
United States of America

Acknowledgments

In addition to our fellow authors, we also wish to express appreciation to Dr. Stephen Gibson, whose invaluable editorial assistance made this project possible.

Table of Contents

Preface	A Time for Affirmation 7	
	By Dr. Michael Avery	
Chapter 1	God's Book 9	
	By Dr. Stephen Gibson	
Chapter 2	Who Is God? 17	
	By Rev. Larry D. Smith	
Chapter 3	The Trinity 25	
	By Dr. Mark Bird	
Chapter 4	To Be Human 37	
	By Rev. Ben Durr, Jr.	
Chapter 5	Sin: The Root of Every Problem 45	
	By Dr. Philip Brown	
Chapter 6	The Real Jesus 63	
	By Dr. Mark Bird	
Chapter 7	The Holy Spirit 73	
	By Dr. Mark Bird	
Chapter 8	Satan: Our Chief Enemy 81	
	By Dr. Stephen Gibson	
Chapter 9	Salvation: God's Provision 87	
	By Dr. Philip Brown	

Chapter 10	Salvation: God's Work and Our Response . 95 By Dr. Philip Brown	
Chapter 11	An Introduction to Christian Holiness . . 105 By Dr. Allan Brown	
Chapter 12	Understanding Entire Sanctification. . . 113 By Dr. Allan Brown	
Chapter 13	Steps to Entire Sanctification . . . . 123 By Dr. Allan Brown	
Chapter 14	The Three Pillars of Assurance . . . . . . 133 By Dr. Allan Brown	
Chapter 15	The Church: The Home Where We Belong 145 By Rev. Larry D. Smith	
Chapter 16	Christ's Triumphant Return . . . . 153 By Rev. Richard Miles	
Chapter 17	Heaven: Eternal Life with God . . . . . . 159 By Rev. Richard Miles	
Chapter 18	Eternal Punishment . . . . 165 By Dr. Daniel Glick	
Chapter 19	Final Events . . . . 171 By Dr. Stephen Gibson	
Chapter 20	The Ancient Creeds of the Church 181	
Appendix	Answers to Questions for Study 189	

PREFACE

A Time for Affirmation

I believe . . .

The line of Christians who have stood for their faith with those words spans the centuries and circles the globe. Because of their faith, they are called not only "Christians," but also "Believers."

Christianity is more than a statement of beliefs, but the church must fulfill its responsibility to be the "pillar and ground of the truth."[1] Though we do not approve of the misguided actions and prejudiced attitudes that have sometimes marked doctrinal controversy, yet we realize that the church holds truth worth defending.

Truth that is not affirmed is soon neglected and finally denied. There is no doctrine that is so elementary and so well established that it does not need to be explained and affirmed for a new generation. In every age the church must communicate clearly the "faith once delivered to the saints."

What form does that challenge take today?

Findings from the recent National Study of Youth and Religion in America offer amazing insight. The good news of the survey is twofold. First, *teens like church*. Seventy-five percent of the teens surveyed wanted to attend more religious services than they do. Second, *teens overwhelmingly admire and seek to practice the religion and faith of their parents*. Both of these findings buck the conventional wisdom about teens.

However, the good news is overshadowed by the bad news that *almost no teenagers from any religious background could articulate the most basic beliefs about their faith*. Only four percent of those involved in one-on-one interviews mentioned repentance in con-

---

[1] 1 Timothy 3:15.

nection with their faith; three percent mentioned the resurrection; and only one percent mentioned discipleship. How did most describe their faith? Forty-two percent described their faith in terms of "personally feeling, getting or being made happy." Most of these kids have been shaped by a "consumer theology" that casts the gospel in terms of "benefits derived." They see God as a generous grandpa primarily concerned with their happiness.

The alarming news is that the majority of these young people are excited about a faith that is neither biblical nor saving. The exciting news is that we have a sacred opportunity to teach a generation of young people anxious to learn about their faith.

In response to this opportunity, the Bible faculty of God's Bible School and College has written *I Believe* to restate the basic Christian doctrines that we hold as most important. The simple style of presentation, explaining not only what we believe but why we believe it, will make this book useful for anyone who has a keen interest in truth. The writers have systematically covered the main themes of Christian theology from a Wesleyan perspective. While there is much more that could be said on every topic, the essentials will be found here.

We have sought to affirm only what Scripture affirms. This approach comes from our deep commitment to the authority of Scripture as the absolute, timeless truth revealed by God. We are guided by the tradition of the church and the best reasoning of spiritual thinkers, but we must also go back to Scripture itself for evaluation and correction of our ideas, making sure that the fountain of Scripture is the source of the teachings that guide us.

Biblical doctrine is God's truth revealed. When we expound the truth of Scripture we can be sure that our words will be empowered and made fruitful by the anointing of the Holy Spirit. God's word is a foundation on which we can build for time and eternity.

May God help us to teach a new generation of Christians so that they can stand with the church of the ages in the great affirmation, "I believe."

Michael Avery, President
God's Bible School and College

1

God's Book

One of the ancient philosophers supposedly said that if there is a meaning to the universe, only the gods could tell us what it is, for only they can stand outside the world and see it as a whole. That philosopher may not have believed that such revelation would ever occur, but he was right to recognize the limits of human reasoning to arrive at truth.

Christians believe that God, the Creator of the world, has spoken. We believe that He has revealed Himself and the purpose of His creation. He has revealed His truth in several ways.

The Meaning of Revelation

General revelation is what we can understand about God by looking at His creation. We see evidence that the universe has design, we see that there are natural laws put in place, and we see significance in the nature of humanity. The fact that we can reason, appreciate beauty, and tell the difference between right and wrong (though not infallibly) shows us that our Creator must possess those abilities to a higher degree.[1]

General revelation prepares the way for special revelation. It shows that God is a person,[2] and therefore able to speak to His rational creatures. It shows people to be sinful and "without excuse" before their Creator.

---

[1] Some of the truth that can be known of God by general revelation is summarized in Romans 1:20: "For since the creation of the world His invisible attributes are clearly seen, being understood by the things that are made, even His eternal power and God-head, so that they are without excuse."

[2] We are not saying that God is a human, but that He is a person, able to think, will, and speak, instead of some impersonal force.

Special revelation has occurred in the inspiration of the Bible and in the incarnation of Christ. Special revelation explains the condition that general revelation shows us to be in: fallen and guilty. Special revelation describes God, explains the Fall and sin, and shows the way to be reconciled to God.

The Bible's Claim

The Bible brings to us God's special revelation. The Bible claims to be the Word of God. In the Old Testament, statements that specific messages came from God are made more than 3,000 times, often expressed as simply as, "Then the Lord spoke . . ."[3] Jesus considered the Old Testament to be inspired by God.[4] Writers of the New Testament considered the Old Testament to be from God.[5] Writers of the New Testament considered the New Testament writings to be inspired by God.[6]

Some people brush these claims aside, saying that a book is not proved to be inspired simply because it claims to be. They say that the same is claimed for the books of other religions. However, the Bible's claim must be taken seriously because evidence supports the Bible's claim.

The Bible was written by more than forty authors, most of whom were not acquainted with most of the others, over a period of 1,500 years. What would we normally expect of such a book? We would assume that it would have all kinds of mistakes and contradictions. But consider the following facts about the Bible. Thousands of geographical sites mentioned in the Bible have been located; thousands of historical events and individuals mentioned in the Bible are confirmed by secular history; never has any discovery refuted a biblical statement; and never does the Bible contradict itself. Such statements are not true of any other book ever written. Evidence supports the Bible's claim to be inspired by God.

---

[3] For examples, see Numbers 34:1, 35:1, and 35:9.
[4] Matthew 5:17-18, John 10:35, Mark 12:36.
[5] Acts 3:18, 2 Peter 1:20-21, 2 Timothy 3:16.
[6] 1 Corinthians 14:37, 2 Peter 3:16.

Defining Inspiration

What do we mean by inspiration? Sometimes people feel like they have been inspired when they have great ideas, but the Bible means more than that when it claims to be inspired by God.

> Never has any discovery refuted a biblical statement.

"All Scripture is given by inspiration of God, and is profitable for doctrine, for reproof, for correction, for instruction in righteousness."[7]

The phrase "given by inspiration of God" means "breathed by God." Though Scripture flowed from pens in human hands, the emphasis of this verse is that the Bible came from God. It is because it is from God that it is reliable for doctrine, etc. It is better than the best that men could do.

"Knowing this first, that no prophecy of Scripture is of any private interpretation, for prophecy never came by the will of man, but holy men of God spoke as they were moved by the Holy Spirit."[8]

These verses in 2 Peter say literally that writers were *carried along* by the Holy Spirit. Their accuracy did not depend on their own knowledge. The fact that they were moved, or carried, by the Holy Spirit in their writing, shows that the reliability of the writing ultimately depended on God. The Bible is reliable if God is.

We could say that inspiration is the supernatural work in which God revealed Himself and brought that revelation to written form. The Bible is the end product of inspiration.

What Was Inspiration Like?

Sometimes people wonder how inspiration worked. How did God communicate His truth and make sure it was recorded

---

[7] 2 Timothy 3:16.
[8] 2 Peter 1:21-22.

accurately? The first fact we should notice about God's style of revelation is that it has variety. He is not limited to a certain method. He spoke "at various times and in different ways."[9]

> **The Bible is reliable if God is.**

Sometimes God spoke with an audible voice.[10] At other times He gave dreams or visions.[11] Perhaps the part of Scripture that came most directly from God into print was the covenant with Israel that was "written with the finger of God."[12] Other sections of Scripture seem to have been dictated, for major passages in Exodus, Leviticus, and Numbers come after the statement, "And the Lord spoke to Moses, saying." It may be that many of the prophets' messages were also preached verbatim as God gave them.

Not all of Scripture was dictated. The human authors were not always mere secretaries, copying down what God told them. A problem with assuming that it was all dictated the same way is that we see differences in personalities and writing styles among various writers. For example, Paul's style is very different from Peter's. Our view of inspiration needs to include God's use of the human writers' personalities, vocabularies, writing styles, education, and historical research.

Some people think that God just gave the ideas that He wanted to communicate, and the human writer explained them the best he could, inevitably making mistakes in details. That view does not fit the Bible's description of inspiration. The Bible describes the authors' being "carried" in their writing, so we know that they were not left to write on their own, making mistakes.

---

9 Hebrews 1:1.
10 As in the speaking of the 10 commandments in Exodus 19-20.
11 For examples of revelation by vision, see Daniel 7 and 8, and most of the book of Revelation.
12 **Deuteronomy 9:10** "Then the Lord delivered to me two tablets of stone written with the finger of God, and on them were all the words which the Lord had spoken to you on the mountain from the midst of the fire on the day of the assembly."

Also, since God revealed Himself most in the history recorded in the Bible (and history takes up most of the Bible), if the details are not accurate, we do not have a reliable revelation of God. Therefore, for our view of inspiration to match the biblical description, we must realize that God guided the writing so that it was completely accurate.

The right view of inspiration is that God inspired the whole person, using the human writer's imagination and personality to express divine truth, and superintending the writing process to provide total accuracy.

Terms Used to Defend the Bible's Total Accuracy

- **Inspired:** That the Bible is inspired means that it is the Word of God, given by His revelation. This term was originally sufficient to assert the full reliability and accuracy of the Bible, but now some people who say that they believe the Bible is inspired deny that it is completely accurate. The following terms have come into use to defend essential aspects of inspiration.

- **Infallible:** This term means "cannot fail." When we say that the Bible is infallible, we mean that it can be trusted and will never mislead us. The Bible is infallible not only in its doctrinal statements, but in every statement it makes.

- **Inerrant:** This term means "without error." The Bible is accurate in every statement that it makes. Since God would never lie or make a mistake,[13] and the Bible is God's word, we can be sure that it is without mistake. If a person says that the Bible may have mistakes because humans were involved in its writing, he is overlooking the description of inspiration in 2 Peter 1:21-22: the writers were "carried along" by the Holy Spirit. The biblical, historical view of inspiration is that all of

---

[13] **Titus 1:2** "In hope of eternal life, which God, Who cannot lie, promised before the world began."

the Bible is inspired, even to the very words, and therefore without error.[14]

What about errors in copying and translation?

We do not still have the original manuscripts written by Paul, Isaiah, or Moses. Among the thousands of ancient, handwritten copies that we have, there are slight differences, and we cannot always know exactly what the original wording was. However, the differences are so slight that there is no doctrine made questionable because of them.

Some would consider the doctrine of inerrancy valueless since we no longer have inerrant copies. However, if we have reason to believe that the originals were inerrant, then by comparing the copies we have, we know that the possibility of error is limited to a few insignificant details. We have a Bible that we can trust.

Because the Bible Is God's Word . . .

- ◆ It will never be outdated or irrelevant. It applies to all people, in all places and times.

- ◆ It is the guide for discerning God's will, since God will never contradict Himself or change His mind.

- ◆ It is our guide for getting the best out of life, since God, our Maker, gave it as directions for us.

- ◆ It contains everything we need to know to be saved and to walk in relationship with God.

- ◆ The Holy Spirit illuminates God's word for our understanding and directs us to obey it.

---

[14] **Matthew 5:18** "For assuredly, I say to you, till heaven and earth pass away, one jot or one tittle will by not means pass from the law till all is fulfilled." This statement of Jesus shows that He considered the Bible to be the Word of God even down to the very letters. That leaves no room for error, since God does not make mistakes or lie.

Is the Bible finished?

From the time that the last apostle died, the church has considered the Bible a finished book. It is important to realize that the church did not merely select writings to call Scripture; instead, they recognized that certain writings were inspired by God and had Scriptural authority. The writings that were recognized as Scripture met qualifications that no later writings could meet.

For Old Testament books, the church kept the writings that Israel had preserved as Scripture. New Testament Scripture was recognized by the following qualifications: historical tie to the apostles, self-authenticating quality, unanimous church acceptance, respectful use of the Old Testament, and usefulness for resistance of heresy.

God still speaks, but can something be added to the Bible now? It is not possible for any new writing to meet the qualifications that led to the inclusion of the original Scriptures. For example, no new writing can be tied to the apostles, for they are not still with us. Neither could any new writing be accepted by the whole church worldwide.

Actually, we can see that Scripture is complete and sufficient for salvation and Christian living.[15] If someone tried to add something good to Scripture, he would find it there already. If he tried to add something defective, he would find it contradicted. The people who claim to be receiving new revelation should instead spend their time studying the revelation God has already given. They will find there all that they need and be guarded from error.

---

15 **1 Timothy 3:14, 16** "... the Holy Scriptures, that are able to make you wise for salvation ... That the man of God may be perfect, thoroughly equipped for every good work."

> **I Believe...**
> The Bible is the Word of God, inspired, infallible, and inerrant. It includes everything that we need to know in order to be saved and to walk in relationship with God.

Questions for Study

1. What is general revelation?
2. In what forms has God given special revelation?
3. What truths are revealed by special revelation that are not revealed by general revelation?
4. What claim does the Bible make for itself?
5. Why is the Bible "profitable for doctrine, for reproof, for correction, for instruction in righteousness"?
6. What description does the Bible give of inspiration that assures us that the writers were kept from making mistakes?
7. What are some various methods God used for inspiration?
8. Most simply put, what do we mean when we say that the Bible is inspired?
9. What does it mean that the Bible is infallible?
10. What does it mean that the Bible is inerrant?

Recommended Reading

Dockery, David S. *Christian Scripture*. Nashville: Broadman and Holman, 1995.

Hendrix, Howard. *Living by the Book*. Chicago: Moody Press, 1991.

2

Who Is God?

God is the noblest thought that ever can cross our minds, confronting us with eternal mystery and ultimate reality. Close your eyes for a moment, shut out every other thought, and concentrate upon the reality of God. It will bring an immediate sense of awe and reverence—a solemn hush to the soul. For we come face to face with our own beginning and our end and with what really is important and what is not. That is why Frederick W. Faber wrote these lines:

O utter but the name of God

Down in your heart of hearts,

And see how from the world at once

All tempting light departs!

> **He is distinct from all else that exists.**

Who is God? A.W. Tozer showed the importance of this question when he said, "I believe there is scarcely an error in doctrine or a failure in applying Christian ethics that cannot be traced finally to imperfect and ignoble thoughts of God."[1] Jesus told the Samaritan woman at the well that a problem with the Samaritans' worship was that they did not know whom they worshiped. A man's concept of God shapes his most important characteristics and forms the foundation of his entire religion. There can be no more serious error than to be wrong about what God is like.

But who is God, and what is He like? Obviously, all comparisons are inadequate, for He is infinitely beyond and above us.

---

1 *The Knowledge of the Holy*, 10.

Not even the Bible gives us a formal definition of Him or proofs of His existence, but everywhere it simply assumes His being and His power. Genesis tells us how God made the heavens and the earth; the sun, the moon, and the stars; vegetation and animal life; and finally human beings. The first lesson of Scripture is very clear: God is the Creator of all that is. Thus He is distinct from all else that exists, for He is not part of His creation.

But throughout the Bible are many other statements about God. Theologians have carefully summarized the biblical data in lists of God's attributes or personal characteristics. We can never master these with our imperfect understanding, of course; and in one of his hymns, Charles Wesley informs us that God's attributes are numberless. Yet, as A. W. Tozer has reminded us, a reverent study of what we know of them may for the enlightened Christian be a sweet, absorbing, spiritual exercise. Thus we consider the following statements about God. They are all based on His disclosure of Himself in the Bible, and for that reason we can be sure that they are true.

Some Attributes of God

- **God is Personal.** This means that He is a real, living person with intellect, feeling, and will. He is not the sum of the laws of nature or an impersonal force like electricity or gravity. He creates, acts, knows, wills, plans, and speaks. The fact that He is personal makes it possible for us to have a relationship with Him.

- **God is a Spirit.** "God is Spirit; and those who worship Him must worship in spirit and truth."[2] The fact that He is spirit provides the basis for our spiritual communion with Him and our worship of Him. The fact that He is spirit is one reason that He forbade us to make any physical image of Him.

- **God is Eternal.** There was never a time when He did not exist, and there will never be a time when He will not exist; God has no beginning and no end. A name that He has

---

2 John 4:24.

revealed is, I AM WHO I AM;[3] and He is described by John as the one who is, and who was, and who is to come, the Almighty.[4] From everlasting to everlasting, He is God.[5]

➡ **God is a Trinity.** The doctrine of the Trinity comes from the fact that the Bible says there is one God, yet refers to three distinct persons as God. There is only one God, but in His nature are three persons. Though we cannot fully understand the Trinity, it is not illogical, for we are not saying that there are three yet one of the same thing. There is one God, existing as three persons. The Father, Son, and Holy Spirit possess together all the attributes of deity, so that each of them may properly be called God.[6]

➡ **God is All-Powerful.** He is able to do whatever He wishes. "Our God is in heaven; He does whatever He pleases."[7] He has no limits except that He never acts contrary to His holy nature and always carries out what He has promised to do. Nothing is difficult or challenging for God. "The Lord God omnipotent reigns."[8] This is encouraging, for we know that in the midst of our struggles, He is "able to do exceeding abundantly above all that we ask or think, according to the power that works in us . . . ."[9]

➡ **God is Present Everywhere.** There is no place where He is not, and nothing happens that He does not see. "Thus says the Lord, heaven is My throne, and earth is My footstool."[10] "Can anyone hide himself in secret places, so I shall not see him? says the Lord. Do I not fill heaven and earth? says the Lord."[11] This assures us that God knows our temptations and our problems. But it also reminds us that no one can ever be where

---

[3] Exodus 3:14.
[4] Revelation 1:8.
[5] Psalm 90:2.
[6] For further information on the deity of the Son and Holy Spirit, see chapters 6 and 7.
[7] Psalm 115:3.
[8] Revelation 19:6.
[9] Ephesians 3:20.
[10] Isaiah 66:1.
[11] Jeremiah 23:24.

He is not, or sin where He cannot see. All things are naked and opened to His eyes.[12]

➡ **God Knows Everything.** "His understanding is infinite."[13] There is no process of learning for Him, for He knows everything. God has never learned anything from anyone, and there is nobody that can advise Him.[14] God knows the future and therefore is never surprised or unprepared for anything that happens.[15]

➡ **God is Unchanging.** There was never a time when He became God, and He will never cease to be God. Every good gift . . . is from . . . the Father of lights, with whom there is no variation or shadow of turning.[16] In His being and nature, and in His attributes and purposes, God never changes.[17] He always loves what is right, and He always hates what is wrong. The Eternal God who revealed Himself as the I AM to Moses is the I AM of today, infinite, eternal, and unchangeable in His being, wisdom, power, holiness, justice, goodness, and truth. He is always the same, and His years shall have no end.[18]

> **God is the absolute standard of all moral perfection.**

➡ **God is Holy.** God's holiness is the summation of what He is, and He has described Himself primarily as holy. He is the absolute standard of all moral perfection. His actions are marked by the presence of all goodness and by the absence of all evil, and can never be

---

12 Hebrews 4:13.
13 Psalm 147:5.
14 Isaiah 40:13-14 "Who has directed the Spirit of the Lord, or as His counselor has taught Him? With whom did He take counsel, and who instructed Him, and taught Him in the path of justice? Who taught Him knowledge, and showed Him the way of understanding?"
15 Psalm 139:4 "For there is not a word on my tongue, but behold, O Lord, You know it altogether."
16 James 1:17.
17 Malachi 3:6.
18 Psalm 102:27.

otherwise. The prophet Isaiah repeatedly referred to God as "The Holy One of Israel." The angels cry "Holy, Holy, Holy" before Him continually.[19] The holiness of God was the theme of worship: "Let them praise thy great and awesome name; for it is holy."[20] God's holiness showed man's inadequacy to serve and worship without being transformed by grace.[21] He desires that we be holy like Himself. "But as He who called you is holy, you also be holy in all your conduct; because it is written, be holy; for I am holy."[22]

➡ **God is Righteous.** His righteous actions flow from His holiness and are always fair and right. Here is the foundation of His holy law, by which He has given the perfect standard of our duties to Him and to others. That law is unbending, and He administers it justly, always rewarding those who obey it and punishing those who break it, unless they meet His conditions for receiving mercy. This comforts those who are suffering and oppressed, but it also warns us that no one will ever get away with doing wrong. "The judgments of the Lord are true and righteous altogether."[23] He "will render to each one according to his deeds."[24] "We shall all stand before the judgment seat of Christ."[25]

➡ **God is Love.** He is our gracious Heavenly Father who so loved the world that He gave His only-begotten Son that whoever believes in Him should not perish but have everlasting life.[26] In spite of our sin and rebellion, He reaches out to us in mercy, inviting us to come to Him through Jesus, whom He has provided as the atoning sacrifice for our sins.[27] It is at the cross where God most fully shows us His heart, which overflows with love and pity for us. God is love; and he who

---

19 Isaiah 6:3.
20 Psalm 99:3.
21 Isaiah 6:5.
22 1Peter 1:15-16.
23 Psalm 19:9.
24 Romans 2:6.
25 Romans 14:10.
26 John 3:16.
27 1 John 2:2.

abides in love abides in God, and God in him."[28] "In this is love, not that we loved God, but that He loved us and sent His Son to be the propitiation for our sins."[29] In His relationship with every person, God is always loving and never unkind.

In contrast to God, everything else appears cheap and unimportant, and only He seems worthy of our pursuit. This is because He has made us for Himself, as St. Augustine reminds us; and we shall never be at rest until we find our rest in Him. It is impossible to find lasting satisfaction anywhere but in God, who has revealed Himself in the splendor of nature, in the truth of Scripture, and in the person of His Son Jesus Christ. His eternal purpose is to bring us to worship Him above all things, trust in Him as our Heavenly Father, and do His will in every area of our lives. "The fear of the Lord is the beginning of wisdom, and the knowledge of the Holy One is understanding."[30]

I Believe . . .
God is a Spirit all-powerful, all-knowing, present everywhere, unchanging, holy, righteous, and loving. He reveals Himself in order to bring us into a loving and fulfilling relationship with Himself.

Questions for Study

1. What is the most serious error possible?
2. What is Scripture's first lesson about God?
3. What are God's personal characteristics called?
4. Name the attribute of God that matches each statement:
    A. God does not have a physical body.
    B. God has always existed.

---

[28] 1 John 4:16.
[29] 1 John 4:10.
[30] Proverbs 9:10.

C. God is not an impersonal force.

D. God's nature will always be the same.

E. God can do whatever He wishes.

F. God sees everything.

G. God sent His Son so we could have mercy.

H. God has three persons in His nature.

I. God has absolute moral perfection.

J. God's actions are always fair and just.

K. God is never surprised by anything.

Recommended Reading

Purkiser, W.T., ed. *Exploring Our Christian Faith*. Kansas City, MO: Beacon Hill Press, 1960.

Tozer, A.W. *The Knowledge of the Holy*. New York: Harper and Row, 1961.

3

The Trinity

"**Y**ou *tell us that there are three gods and yet one,*" *the puzzled Irish said when St. Patrick was preaching the gospel to them in the 5th century AD. "How can that be?" The saint bent down and plucked a shamrock. "Do you not see," he said, "how in this wildflower three leaves are united on one stalk, and will you not then believe that there are indeed three persons and yet one God?"*[1]

Using this illustration from nature, St. Patrick was able to help some of the pagan Celtics to accept the doctrine of the Trinity.

I think an even better illustration of the Trinity is the universe itself (though no illustration is perfect). Isn't it interesting that the *entire* physical *universe* (uni = one) consists of *three and only three* aspects—space, time, and matter? If you were to take away any of these three, you would no longer have a universe. Each of those three also consists of three aspects.

SPACE consists of length, width, and height—three in one. If you were to take away any of these dimensions, you would no longer have space.

TIME consists of past, present, and future—three in one. If you were to take away any of these aspects, you would no longer have time.

---

1 Encyclopedia Britannica Online, "Saint Patrick."

MATTER consists of *energy* in *motion* producing *phenomena*—three in one. If there were no energy, there could be no motion or phenomena. If there were no motion, there would be no energy or phenomena. If there were no phenomena, it would be because there was no energy or motion.[2]

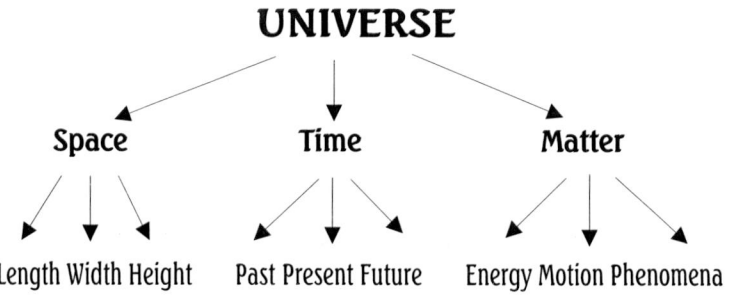

We see this threeness in oneness composing the very fabric of the universe. Why do you suppose the nature of the universe is so trinitarian? Could it be that God made His universe to reflect His trinitarian nature? I believe that God left His fingerprints on the work of His creation, and we see in it a reflection of the Trinity.

So what does the Bible teach about the Trinity? It clearly affirms the existence of *three* distinct Persons that are all identified as the one God of the universe. This is not a contradiction, because we are not saying that God is both one person and three persons. Neither are we saying that God is both one God and three Gods. We are saying that God is one in essence and three in person. Just as the one universe exists as space, time, and matter, the one God exists as the Father, the Son, and the Holy Spirit.

> **Could it be that God made His universe to reflect His trinitarian nature?**

---

[2] See *Trinity in the Universe*, by Nathan Wood, reprinted in 1984 by Kriegel Publications.

The Case for the Trinity

Our belief in the Trinity does not first come from our observation of the universe, but from Scripture. The following premises[3] are all taught in the Bible, and form the basis of the doctrine of the Trinity.

➡ **Premise 1: There is only one God.**

"Hear O Israel, the Lord our God is One Lord" (Deut. 6:4).

"For I am God, and there is no other; I am God, and there is none like Me" (Isaiah 46:9).

➡ **Premise 2: The Father, the Son, and the Holy Spirit are all identified in Scripture as God.**

". . . God the Father . . ." (Gal. 1:1).

". . . the Word was God . . . the Word became flesh" (John 1:1, 14).

". . . why has Satan filled your heart to lie to the Holy Spirit? . . . You have not lied to men but to God." (Acts 5:3-4).[4]

➡ **Premise 3: These three each relate to one another and to the world as distinct Persons.**

In Mark 1:10-11, Jesus is baptized, the Holy Spirit descends like a dove, and a voice from Heaven says, "You are My beloved Son, in whom I am well pleased." We see here that the Father, Son, and Holy Spirit could not be the same person; they are each acting in different roles at the same time.

Toward the end of His ministry, Jesus said He would ask the Father to send to us "another Helper"—the Holy Spirit (John 15:26). Do you see the three distinct persons involved in this request?

---

[3] In a logical argument, the premises are the statements from which the conclusion follows. In a valid logical argument, if the premises are true, then the conclusion is true.

[4] See chapters 6 and 7 for discussion of the Son's deity and the Holy Spirit's deity and personality.

Conclusion: The one true God of the Bible has revealed Himself to exist in three distinct persons: Father, Son, and Holy Spirit. God is one in nature, but three in person.

So, though the word *Trinity* does not appear in the Bible, the doctrine of the Trinity is based on clear Scriptural statements.

This biblical doctrine has been taught by the church since the apostles. Below is a diagram that the church has used over the centuries to describe the Trinity.

Traditional Diagram of the Trinity

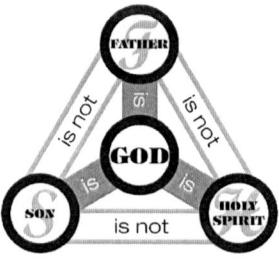

The Doctrine of the Trinity Is Essential.

Some say that it is not important to believe the doctrine of the Trinity, but that is wrong. The doctrine of the Trinity underlies key teachings that are essential to the gospel. For example, those who deny the Trinity usually deny that Jesus is God. But if the Jesus you believe in is not God, you don't have a Jesus who can save you!

Also, if we deny that the Father, Son, and Holy Spirit are distinct, we deny God His natural personal or relational characteristics. For instance, God would not be a loving God from all eternity if He had to wait until He created in order to love anyone. But if God is more than one person, these Persons could love each other from all eternity. It is important to believe in this relational God (who exists in self-giving love) because it affects the way we relate to one another, as well as to God.

The Father, Son, and Holy Spirit Are *Persons* Living in Relationship.

The Father, Son, and Holy Spirit are not impersonal entities. They each possess personhood and from eternity past have lived in personal relationship with each other. We call them persons because they live in relationship with one another. Each member of the Trinity can refer to Himself as "I" and can communicate to another member of the Trinity as "You." Though the Father, Son, and Holy Spirit are one God, they are distinct enough to love one another, to give to one another, to communicate with one another, and to live for one another. This makes them *Persons*.

> The Son is eternally self-existent as God

➡ The Son's Relationship to His Father

Specifically, how does the Son relate to the Father? From all eternity the Son has been the Father's beloved and "only begotten Son."[5] Jesus said that the Father had granted Him as Son "to have life in Himself," just "as the Father has life in Himself."[6] The Son is eternally self-existent as God, and is of the same nature as the Father, yet His existence is from the Father. Eternally, the Son has related to the Father as a Son, and the Father has related to the Son as a Father, though not in a physical sense.

Since the Son has eternally related to the Father as a Son, He is eternally submissive to the Father. He functions in a subordinate role. This is why Jesus said, "My Father is greater than I."[7]

---

[5] John 3:16.
[6] John 5:26.
[7] John 14:28.

It is important to stress that Christ's eternal submission to His Father does not in any way diminish His value as God the Son. It is like a woman's relationship with her husband. A woman's submission to her husband does not diminish her value as a person; she is equal to her husband in essence. Likewise, though Jesus has a lower position of authority than the Father has, He is equal to the Father in His basic nature. He is to be worshiped and glorified on the same level as the Father. Jesus said that all should honor Him "just as they honor the Father."[8]

➡ The Holy Spirit's Relationship to the Father and Son

> Though the Spirit proceeds from the Father, He is equal to the Father and the Son, and is to be equally honored.

The word used to show the relationship between the Holy Spirit and the other members of the Trinity is *proceeding*. In John 15:26, Jesus said that He would *send* to us the Holy Spirit, "which *proceeds* from the Father." Though the Spirit proceeds from the Father, He is equal to the Father and the Son, and is to be equally honored. Keep in mind that this proceeding and sending is happening between three Persons living in loving relationship with each other.

➡ Structure in the Trinity

Let me emphasize that the Father, Son, and Holy Spirit have always existed in a structure of relationships. The Father is the Head, then the Son, then the Spirit. These three timeless and equal Persons have positions of authority based on their relationships with each other. This structure of authority is reflected in the family and in the church. Like the Trinity, all the members of the family and in the church have equal value, but not all have the same position of authority.

---

8   John 5:23.

➡ Protecting the Unity of God

The three persons of the Trinity are not to be considered separate individuals. The unity of their being means that they are of the same essence *and* that the three persons permeate one another, indwell one another, and share their attributes with one another.[9] The Father, the Son, and the Holy Spirit experience mutual indwelling in a way that humans could not.

We humans are persons *and* individuals since we are each individual beings. God is three persons, yet only one being.[10] To help protect the biblical concept of the unity of God:

- **Don't speak of the members of the Trinity as individuals.**

- **Don't say that there are three *people* in the Trinity. That makes the Father, the Son, and the Spirit sound like human individuals.**

- **Don't say there are three *personalities* in the Trinity, though they each have personality.**

- **Don't speak of the persons in the Trinity as "separate." Use the word *distinct*. We don't want to imply there are three separate individuals in the Trinity.**

We Reflect God's Personhood and Relations

The Trinity (the three-personal God) is the source of our personhood. God made us in His image as persons—having the capacity to relate to one another and to God. We have a mind, a will, and emotions so that we can have that capacity.

---

9   The ancient church described this interpersonal permeation as "perichoresis." *Perichoresis* means "mutual indwelling." There is threeness in oneness because of this mutual personal permeation.

10 The term *individual* suggests singularity of being, whereas the term *person* (which signifies the ability to have relationship) would allow for a plurality of persons in one being. Of course, there are only three persons who are not also individuals; these persons are the three members of the Trinity. If these persons were also individuals (separate beings), there would not be one God, but three. Belief in three gods is a heresy called Tritheism.

➡ Individually We Are Incomplete

After God created Adam, He said, "It is not good that man should be alone."[11] Then He made Eve. Adam was incomplete without Eve because, without her, he didn't have another human to relate to. In fact, one scripture suggests that Adam and Eve *together* reflected God's image: "So God created man in His own image, in the image of God He created him, male and female He created them."[12] There seems to be something about the relationship between Adam and Eve that made them together reflect the image of God more than Adam would have by himself. Think about what that means for us. We too are not functioning as whole persons unless we are in relationship with others, as the persons of the Trinity are. We don't have to get married like Adam did (in heaven, no one will be married, yet we will still be persons), but we do need to have fellowship with others. When we get to heaven, we will deepen our personal relationships with God and with each other.

➡ Relating to Reflect the Image of God

There is a wonderful comparison between the nature of God and the nature of the church. Within both God and the church, there is unity and diversity. According to 1 Cor. 12, the body of Christ is a unity composed of many parts functioning together for a purpose. Can you see how the body of Christ reflects the image of God? The Apostle Paul expected all the various members of the church to grow together as one in Christ. Paul prayed that we would:

> "grow up in all things into Him who is the head—Christ—from whom the whole body, joined and knit together by what every joint supplies, according to the effective working by which every part does its share, causes growth of the body for the edifying of itself in love."[13]

---

[11] Genesis 2:18.
[12] Genesis 1:27.
[13] Ephesians 4:15-16.

This verse means that all of us are to use our gifts and abilities to help each other grow together in the unity of Christ. If your pastor ever asks you to join a discipleship group, there is a reason. God's will is that all of us reflect His relational nature by personally helping each other grow in grace. There is "no holiness apart from social holiness" (as John Wesley said). Spiritual growth occurs in community (in fellowship and intimacy with other believers). This reflects the social nature of God.

If the members of the Trinity have for eternity lived in self-giving love for each other, shouldn't we live in loving relationships with others? We were made in the image of God as social, relational beings. Should we not then focus on others rather than ourselves? Should we not emphasize community more than our individuality? I believe God will bless us as we attempt more fully to reflect His triune image in our relationships with others.

> **There is no holiness apart from social holiness.**

Trinitarian Worship

What does it mean to worship as a Trinitarian? We certainly do not want be unitarian in the way we worship. A unitarian would pray only to the Father, neglecting the Son's and the Spirit's roles in worship. Trinitarian worship recognizes that we come to the Father with the aid of the Spirit and on the basis of the atoning work of the Son. As Trinitarians, we are to pray to the Father, in the Spirit, through the Son.

An important goal of worship is for us to become caught up into the dynamic life of God, into the love relationship that the members of the Trinity have for each other. Think particularly of the love that exists between the Father and the Son. Also think of what Christ did on the cross so that we could experience that love. The Father and Son live in wonderful communion with each other, and because of the Son's atoning work, the Spirit is able to help us participate in that fervent love relationship.

As Trinitarians, we not only pray to the Father, in the Spirit, through the Son, but we also pray to the Father, to the Son, and to the Spirit. Each of the members of the Trinity is to be adored, to be verbally glorified, for they are all God and must be equally honored. Trinitarian worship brings glory to each member of the Trinity equally, recognizing the role each plays in our salvation.

> Almighty and everlasting God,
> You have given us your servants grace
> by the confession of a true faith
> to acknowledge the glory of the eternal Trinity,
> and in the power of the divine Majesty
> to worship the unity.
> Keep us steadfast in this faith,
> that we may evermore be defended from all adversaries:
> through Jesus Christ our Lord,
> who lives and reigns with you and the Holy Spirit,
> one God, now and forever. Amen.[14]

I Believe...
The Father, Son, and Holy Spirit are the one, infinite, transcendent God. The three members of the Trinity have eternally dwelt in self-giving love for each other. The relations in the Trinity help us to understand how we as persons are to relate to God and to one another.

---

14 *Book of Common Prayer.*

Questions for Study

1. What are some ways that creation illustrates the nature of God?

2. What three biblical premises are the foundation for the doctrine of the Trinity?

3. What is the structure of the relationships within the Trinity?

4. What are some human relationships that should reflect the relationships of the Trinity?

5. What should human relationships be like, based on our reflection of the image of the Trinity?

6. What does it mean to worship as a Trinitarian?

Recommended Reading

Morey, Robert. *The Trinity: Evidences and Issue*. Iowa Falls, IA: Word Bible Publishers, 1996.

White, James. *The Forgotten Trinity: Recovering the Heart of Christian Belief*. Minneapolis: Bethany House Publishers, 1998.

4

To Be Human

My son David once wrote a science-fiction essay, a story that was to be read to his English composition class. He asked me to proofread it, and when I did I got caught up in the plot. His paper was about human cloning. It described a boy named "David" (his name, in case you missed it) who had made a clone of himself years ago. He then made a slave out of his clone. David could sleep in every day; he forced his clone to go to school, and no one knew the difference! He made his clone clean his room and, you guessed it, it even did David's homework! The paper concluded with a passionate plea from the clone to the class asking them to rescue him from the cruel dominance of his genetic counterpart who was, at the moment, sitting at home taking it easy!

The subject of human cloning does raise some very difficult and intriguing questions, not the least of which is, Who would the clone really be? Would the clone have its own identity? These questions drive us back to yet another more basic study: Who are we really? In what ways are we all the same? What gives us our identity? What does it really mean to be a human being?

> **What does it really mean to be a human being?**

Those are some big questions to tackle, but the starting place is Genesis 1:26. There we read: "Then God said, 'Let Us make man in Our image, according to Our likeness.'" There is obviously something special about being part of the human family.

There is something within our make up that is "God-like." Now, we are not God, that's for sure, but there is something "God-like" about us, something that separates us from the rest of the animal world and makes us unique. This reminds me of Psalm 8:5 where the Psalmist rejoices that we have been made "a little lower than the angels" and have been "crowned with glory and honor."

> **There is something "God-like" about us.**

This lofty view of mankind is certainly better for our self-esteem than is the doctrine of evolution! If evolution is true, I'm nothing special; I'm only lucky. In evolution I am essentially no more important than my lazy German Shepherd. In evolution there is no significance to life, no purpose, no meaning, nothing special about being a human.

But scripture teaches that you and I were created in the "image of God." What does that mean? Theologians have thought long and hard about this question and have, for the most part, agreed that the following qualities are part of what it means to be created in God's image.

Elements of the Image of God Imparted to Humanity

High on the list is a **moral instinct** that is part of our very nature. Humanity has fallen into sin and marred that basic moral image, but there still remains within each one of us the capacity to understand the concepts of right and wrong. People disagree on what is right or wrong, but the very use of the words "right" and "wrong" points to something that is special in all human beings, a capacity to grasp moral concepts. We possess an inward moral compass.

Secondly, **free will**, or the power of choice, is characteristic of human beings. If I set two bowls of dog food in front of my German Shepherd (which I'm sure would be much to his delight), he would have to choose between the two. Knowing him, he'd probably eat both, but he'd have to choose one bowl before the other. And so there is a sense in which animals may seem to make choices, at least on a lower level. But animals seem not to have the capacity for self-determination. That is, their "choices" are basically on the level of momentary impulse and instinct rather than being deliberate, thought-out decisions that weigh the ethical or practical implications of their actions. Human beings have the ability to make meaningful, life-altering choices.

Thirdly, we have a **creative instinct** that grows out of God's image within us. Our Creator has made us to be creative! I've heard stories about animals (such as an ape) being taught to make strokes on a canvas with a paintbrush. (And I assume that these "paintings" were then sold to gullible art collectors at enormous prices!) But training a monkey to move a brush around on a canvas is a far cry from an idea being nurtured in the human mind and then expressed artistically through a delicate painting.

Creativity is also revealed in music. Music has a marvelous capacity to express our thoughts and feelings, and the ability to communicate ideas creatively and imaginatively through music grows out of this unique image of God within us. Closely related to this, of course, is the use of language, where abstract ideas are converted into meaningful sounds or symbols so they can be successfully transmitted to the minds of other human beings.

The use of language can be something of an art form as a speaker or writer employs various literary techniques such as sarcasm, humor, exaggeration, and word-plays to communicate, instruct, inspire, or persuade others. Animals, such as dogs and birds, may "communicate" through special barks or chirps, but nothing even approaching the complexity of human language is known within the animal kingdom. Creative expression through art, music, and language is our special gift from God; it is part of His personal stamp upon us.

The **capacity to think and reason** is yet another "God-like" capacity. Of course animals also have brains, but from all we are able to tell, animals' "brain activity" does not rise above the level of basic instinct and intuition. Only human beings are capable of thinking critically, of evaluating, conjecturing, and reflecting, then communicating persuasively.

A few months ago I ran across a term in a magazine article that really threw me. The term was "metacognitive reflection." (Try casually dropping that one during a dinner conversation and watch the reactions!) I had no clue what it meant, so I read the article carefully. I found out that the term has to do with "thinking about thinking." Kind of stretches your mind, doesn't it? But think about it. Not only can we think, we can think about thinking. We can analyze thought processes. Not only can we think logically, *we can think about logic*. We can analyze and evaluate the validity of certain thought sequences. Amazing!

> **Not only can we think, we can think about thinking.**

Perhaps the most significant aspect of the image of God is the **capacity for relationship**. We are able to relate to others and to God in a way that no other kind of creature can. For one thing, we all came from Adam and Eve, so we are in a family that includes all human beings. That gives a basis for relationship that even the angels do not have. We also have the ability to share ourselves and to understand others, though of course not without errors. This ability to relate to others is certainly a "God-like" quality.

Writers list some other qualities as aspects of the image of God. One mentions **self-awareness** or self-consciousness. Another identifies **immortality**. We are spirit beings, in addition to being physical beings, and our spirit will live on forever. But the final "image of God" characteristic that I wish to discuss is **our capacity for worship**.

Think about your favorite hymns or worship choruses. "Our God Is an Awesome God," we sing. "How Great Thou Art" is a timeless hymn of intense worship. The Psalmist exclaimed, "Bless the Lord, O my soul! And all that is within me, bless His holy name!"[1] These expressions, and multiplied thousands of others like them, are possible only because something within us called "the image of God" recognizes and responds to the awesome God in whose image we are made!

Three Closing Thoughts

- First, all human beings bear the image of God. I'm thinking here particularly of those unfortunate individuals who are mentally handicapped or who, for some reason, do not appear to possess the ability to reason, to express themselves creatively, to relate to others, or to exercise free will. It would be a grave mistake to presume that these precious ones do not bear the image of God, for they are human beings, and they certainly possess all of the innate capacities of humanity, even if those capacities are thwarted by genetic defects or by the consequences of some accident, and may not be fulfilled in their earthly lives.

- Secondly, it should be recognized that sin has horribly warped and distorted these "God-like" capacities within men and women. Free will, for example, has been so damaged by sin that a person is "bound," a "slave to sin," incapable of doing right except for the grace of God that gives him the desire and ability to choose right. Artistic expression can reveal a wicked heart and can be a tool of Satan, even though the basic gift itself comes from God. But we can also rejoice that sin, because of the intervention of grace, has not completely obliterated the image of God within us. And we further rejoice that, touched by grace, the image of God which we all bear can be renewed, developed, and expressed for the glory of our loving Creator!

- Finally, let us observe that the characteristics of the image of God imparted to us make it possible for us to respond to the

---

[1] Psalm 103:1.

Gospel. Our built-in moral compass makes it possible for grace to awaken our conscience and convict us of sin. Free will restored by grace working in us makes it possible for us to "choose whom we will serve." Through our creative instincts we can bring glory and honor to our God, and, employing reason, we can understand something of God and His ways. The quest to understand God then unfolds into worship as we become increasingly aware of the absolute awesomeness of our Creator who has so graciously "crowned us with glory and honor!"

> I Believe . . .
> Man is created in the "image and likeness of God," giving us a unique and exalted position among all of God's creation. This "image of God" includes the capacities for morality, free will, creativity, reason, relationship, self-awareness, immortality, and worship.

Questions for Study

1. What does the fact that we are created tell us about ourselves?
2. What are eight elements of the image of God imparted to humanity?
3. What capacity comes from the moral instinct?
4. How is our free will different from the choices animals make?
5. What is metacognitive reflection?
6. Why do mentally handicapped or limited people also possess the image of God?
7. What are two ways that sin has damaged the image of God in humans?

Recommended Reading

Purkiser, W. T., ed. *Exploring Our Christian Faith*. Kansas City, MO: Beacon Hill, 1978.

See chapter 10: "What is Man?" Taylor, Richard S., ed. *Beacon Dictionary ofTheology*. Kansas City, MO: Beacon Hill, 1983. See entries on "Image" (p. 272, by Armor Peisker) and "Divine Image" (p. 170, by Ross Price).

Because Human beings are a special creation of God, we know that . . .

1. God has a purpose for humanity.

Humanism believes people must find their purpose within themselves. Eastern religions see humanity as part of a purposeless cycle. Some pagan religions see people as the insignificant slaves of deity. Christianity sees people as created to give the highest worship to God and to be the objects of God's love. "The chief end of man is to glorify God and enjoy Him forever."

2. God has a design for human life.

The Bible is the manual for the best results.

The rest of creation glorifies God unconsciously. We are to do so consciously and willingly.

3. Humanity is accountable to God.

Since humans have purpose and free will, their Creator will someday evaluate whether or not they have fulfilled their purpose. Reward or punishment will follow.

5

Sin: The Root of Every Problem

Why do we experience pain and suffering? Why do we have to die? Why is there racism, bigotry, and alienation in society? Why do people steal, murder, commit adultery, and get divorced? Why did 9/11 happen? What's the matter with the world, anyway?

The answer is sin. The root of every problem in our universe is sin. Sin is the reason there is pain and suffering.[1] Sin is the reason we die.[2] Sin is the reason we are alienated from each other and from God.[3] Sin is the reason there is a Hell, and we will go to Hell unless we are saved from our sin.[4]

If the ultimate problem with everything is sin, we need to answer the question, "What is sin?" The word *sin* means "to miss the mark,"[5] and Scripture uses the word *sin* in two ways:[6] (1) to refer to any action, attitude, or desire that misses the mark of God's law,[7] and (2) to refer to the principle of corruption we are

---

[1] **Genesis 3:16** "To the woman He said: 'I will greatly multiply your sorrow and your conception; In pain you shall bring forth children; Your desire *shall be* for your husband, And he shall rule over you.'"
[2] **Romans 5:12** "Therefore, just as through one man sin entered the world, and death through sin, and thus death spread to all men, because all sinned."
[3] **Colossians 1:21** "And you, who once were alienated and enemies in your mind by wicked works, yet now He has reconciled."
[4] **Revelation 20:15** "And anyone not found written in the Book of Life was cast into the lake of fire."
[5] The Hebrew and Greek words translated *sin* both mean "to miss the mark."
[6] Wilcox, *Profiles in Wesleyan Theology*, 154.
[7] God's law is a revelation of God's character. Therefore, any offense against God's law is actually an offense against God Himself.

all born with that causes us to miss the mark of God's law. Since sin as a principle is the root of our sinful actions, attitudes, and desires, let's talk about it first.

The Principle of Sin

Theologians use many different terms to refer to the principle of sin. Some of the most common are "inherited depravity," "the nature of sin," "the sin nature," "a bent toward sinning," "inbred sin," and "carnality." The primary terms the Bible uses for this principle are "sin,"[8] the "law of sin,"[9] and "the flesh."[10]

In order to understand how we came to have this law of sin that makes us self-centered,[11] we need to go back to the Garden of Eden. When God created Adam and Eve, He made them so that they were God-centered and enjoyed a right relationship with Him. As a result of their relationship with God, they had spiritual life, they were holy, and they naturally wanted to and were able to please God in everything they did.

When Adam and Eve sinned, they severed their relationship with God. As a result, they became dead spiritually and began to die physically.[12] Their sin made them unholy and unrighteous. That first sin also corrupted and warped their nature so that

---

8 **Romans 7:8** "But sin, taking opportunity by the commandment, produced in me all *manner of evil* desire. For apart from the law sin *was* dead."
9 **Romans 7:23** "But I see another law in my members, warring against the law of my mind, and bringing me into captivity to the law of sin which is in my members."
10 **Galatians 5:17** "For the flesh lusts against the Spirit, and the Spirit against the flesh; and these are contrary to one another, so that you do not do the things that you wish."
11 The Bible does not directly tell us what the sin principle is. In Psalm 53:3 David says, "Every one of them has turned aside; /They have together become corrupt; /*There is* none who does good, /No, not one." Isaiah 53 explains where we have turned to: "All we like sheep have gone astray, we have turned every one to *his own way*" (Isa. 53:6). From passages like these, theologians of every stripe have concluded that an inward turning away from God toward self is at the heart of man's sinful condition.
12 **Romans 5:12** "Therefore, just as through one man sin entered the world, and death through sin, and thus death spread to all men, because all sinned." Death, both spiritual and physical, entered the world only after Adam sinned. This is a major theological reason why the idea that humanity has evolved over millions of years cannot be true. If there was no death before Adam, then the idea that there were millions of years of death and suffering before Adam must be wrong.

instead of being God-centered, they became self-centered. The law of sin is not some "thing" that entered Adam and Eve when they sinned. It is the corruption of their inner spiritual nature that happened when they forfeited their sanctifying, life-giving relationship with God. This corruption of our inner nature that makes us self-centered and naturally inclined to commit sin is called "depravity."

All of Adam and Eve's children (that's us) have received this corruption or depravity.[13] It affects every part of our being, not just our spirit—that is one reason it is called *total depravity*.[14] Paul tells us that our minds have been darkened and become futile.[15] Our minds have been damaged so that we think things will make us happy that will actually destroy and damn us.[16] This is the reason sinful men call evil good and good evil.[17] Not only have our minds been depraved, but our hearts have been blinded.[18] We can't see spiritual truth. Jeremiah tells us our hearts are desperately sick and deceitful.[19] In fact, after the flood God said that "the imagination of man's heart is evil from his youth."[20] Romans 3:10-18 is the classic passage that describes how wicked our inner corruption would make us if it weren't for God's grace hindering it:

> **This is the reason sinful men call evil good and good evil.**

---

13 **Psalm 51:5** "Behold, I was brought forth in iniquity, And in sin my mother conceived me." David doesn't mean that his mother sinned in the act of conceiving him. He means that sin was a part of his nature from the moment of his conception.
14 **Psalm 53:3** "Every one of them has turned aside; They have together become corrupt; There is none who does good, No, not one."
15 **Ephesians 4:17-18** "... You should no longer walk as the rest of the Gentiles walk, in the futility of their mind, having their understanding darkened..."
16 **Philippians 3:19** "Whose end *is* destruction, whose god *is their* belly, and <u>whose glory *is* in their shame</u>—who set their mind on earthly things."
17 **Isaiah 5:20** "Woe to those who call evil good, and good evil; Who put darkness for light, and light for darkness; Who put bitter for sweet, and sweet for bitter!"
18 **Ephesians 4:18** "Having their understanding darkened, being alienated from the life of God, because of the ignorance that is in them, <u>because of the blindness of their heart</u>."
19 **Jeremiah 17:9** "The heart is deceitful above all things, and desperately wicked; who can know it?"
20 Genesis 8:21b.

[10]As it is written: "There is none righteous, no, not one; [11]There is none who understands; There is none who seeks after God. [12]They have all turned aside; They have together become unprofitable; There is none who does good, no, not one." [13]"Their throat is an open tomb; With their tongues they have practiced deceit"; "The poison of asps is under their lips"; [14]"Whose mouth is full of cursing and bitterness." [15]"Their feet are swift to shed blood; [16]Destruction and misery are in their ways; [17]And the way of peace they have not known." [18]"There is no fear of God before their eyes."

That is a terrible picture of how dreadful our inner corruption is. In Adam and Eve's case their first act of sin brought about their inner depravity. In our case, our acts of sin spring from the corruption of our nature we inherited from Adam. Now let's look at what the Bible teaches about acts of sin.

Sin as Missing the Mark of God's Law

The Bible uses the term sin to refer to both unintentional and intentional violations of God's word. However, the word *sin* normally means a willful trangression of a known law of God. When the Bible talks about the believer's freedom from sin, it is *always* talking about freedom from willful sin.[21]

> *Sin* normally means a willful trangression of a known law of God.

The first human[22] sin was Adam and Eve's disobedience to God's command not to eat from the tree of the knowledge of good and evil.[23] Ever since that first sin, all of Adam's children have sinned: "for all have

---

21 The following passages are representative examples of the Bible's commands and expectations that believers live above sins: John 5:14; 8:11, 34; Rom. 6:1-2, 15, 22; Jam. 4:17; 1 John 3:4-9. In each of these passages, both the immediate and broader contexts indicate that by "sin" the authors mean a willful transgression of God's word.
22 Actually, the very first sin was committed by Satan. But his sin didn't bring death into the world. It was Adam's sin that did this. **1 John 3:8** "He who sins is of the devil, for the devil has sinned from the beginning. For this purpose the Son of God was manifested, that He might destroy the works of the devil."
23 **Genesis 3:11** "And He said, 'Who told you that you were naked? Have you eaten from the tree of which I commanded you that you should not eat?'"

sinned."[24] In most of our cases, we have sinned by willfully failing to do what God's word requires us to do or by doing what it tells us not to do.[25]

We most often think of sin as an action, but God has also given us instructions about our attitudes and desires. Attitudes such as pride, rebellion, a fault-finding spirit, bitterness, wrath, and malice are all forbidden by God's word, and attitudes such as thankfulness, kindness, sympathy, and humility are commanded.[26] God's word also forbids desires such as covetousness and lust and commands us to hunger for righteousness and to desire to live honorably.[27]

Human Infirmity

Many people have mistakenly thought that human infirmity or weakness is also sin. This is not true. Scripture never says that physical or mental limitations and deficiencies are sin. For example, spelling mistakes and forgetfulness are not sins. It is true that weaknesses are a result of our fallen condition, but they are not sins. There are several ways we know this. First, in 2 Corinthians 12:9-10, Paul said that he would glory in his infirmities, because God's power would be seen all the more, compensating for them. Paul would not have gloried in sin. Second, Hebrews 4:15 and 5:2 teach us that although Jesus was without sin of any kind, He was beset by human infirmities or weaknesses.[28] These passages show us that infirmities are not sin.

To sum up what we've said so far, every person (except Jesus) born after Adam and Eve comes into the world naturally self-centered and inclined to sin. As a result, all men have sinned and are

---

24 Romans 3:23.
25 **1 John 3:4** "Whoever commits sin also commits lawlessness, and sin is lawlessness." To "commit lawlessness" means to do what the law forbids or to fail to do what the law requires.
26 Prov. 6:16-17; 1 Sam. 15:22-23; Mat. 7:1; Eph. 4:31; 1 Thess. 5:18; Eph. 4:32; 1 Pet. 3:8-9.
27 Exod. 20:17-18; Mat. 5:28; 5:6; Heb. 13:18.
28 **Hebrews 4:15** "For we do not have a High Priest who cannot sympathize with our weaknesses, but was in all *points* tempted as *we are, yet* without sin." **Hebrews 5:2** "He can have compassion on those who are ignorant and going astray, since he himself is also subject to weakness."

coming short of the glory of God.[29] Because of our fallenness, we frequently make mistakes in our opinions, our words, and our actions. However, as long as these mistakes are not violations of God's word, they are not sins.

Sin and Fellowship with Our Holy God

Here's a quick, two-question pop quiz for you: What book in the Bible talks about sin more than any other book? What book in the Bible talks about holiness more than any other book? Did you answer "Leviticus"? If you did, you're right! God gave us the Book of Leviticus to teach us how to live in holy fellowship with Him. You see, our sins have separated us from God, but God was not content to leave us in our sins. God longs to have intimate fellowship with us. There is, however, one basic problem: God is holy, and we are sinful. In the Book of Leviticus God tells us over and over that we must be holy. In fact, the famous passage in 1 Peter 1:15-16 that calls us to holiness is a quotation from Leviticus![30] Since we must be holy to fellowship with our holy God,[31] He had to teach us how serious sin is and how to have it forgiven so that we could be holy. That's why He put Leviticus in the Bible.

> **God longs to have intimate fellowship with us.**

If you read Leviticus carefully you will see that it teaches us both about sin as an inner principle and about sin as an act that misses the mark of God's law. However, it teaches most clearly about sin as an act that violates "the commandments of the LORD,—*something* which ought not to be done."[32] Leviticus teaches us at least three crucial truths about acts of sin.

---

29 Rom. 3:23.
30 **1 Peter 1:15-16** "But as He who called you *is* holy, you also be holy in all *your* conduct, because it is written, 'Be holy, for I am holy.'"
31 **Leviticus 10:3** "And Moses said to Aaron, 'This is what the LORD spoke, saying: "By those who come near Me I must be regarded as holy; And before all the people I must be glorified."'"
32 Leviticus 4:2.

- First, *God is serious about sin*. Do you remember the story of Nadab and Abihu, Aaron's two sons? They sinned by burning incense in the tabernacle with a fire different from the fire God required. As a result fire came out from God's presence and fried them instantly.[33] That's pretty serious! Another thing that teaches us the seriousness of sin is the fact that every sacrificial animal had to die, illustrating that the penalty for sin is death.

- Second, *there must be a blood sacrifice for sin to be forgiven*. The death of the animal was not what provided atonement for sin. The animal's blood had to be shed, because the life of the flesh is in the blood.[34] This was a picture-prophecy of Christ, the Lamb of God, whose blood would be shed for our sins.

- Third, *God views different kinds of sin differently*. This may surprise you, but God required different kinds of sacrifices for different kinds of sinful acts. Leviticus distinguishes two kinds of sinful acts: unintentional acts and intentional acts.

God deals with unintentional acts of sin in Leviticus 4:1-5:6. Unintentional sins are violations of God's word which you did not *intend* to commit or which you committed not knowing that what you were doing was wrong. The examples God gives of involuntary sins include any sin done in ignorance, failure to testify under oath, and involuntarily touching something that is unclean.[35] God required a sin offering to be sacrificed in order for unintentional sins to be atoned. Whenever the person realized he had sinned unintentionally, he had to offer a sin offering for

> **God views different kinds of sin differently.**

---

33 Leviticus 10:1-5.
34 **Leviticus 17:11** "For the life of the flesh *is* in the blood, and I have given it to you upon the altar to make atonement for your souls; for it *is* the blood *that* makes atonement for the soul."
35 See Lev. 4:1, 13, 22; 5:1-3.

forgiveness, and he had to make restitution.[36] In addition to each person's bringing a sin offering whenever he or she sinned unintentionally, every year the High Priest sacrificed sin offerings on the Day of Atonement to atone for the unintentional sins of the nation as a whole.[37]

The second kind of sin in Leviticus is intentional or willful sin. Intentional sin is deliberately doing what you know is wrong. God deals with this kind of sin in Leviticus 6:1-7. The examples God gives of intentional sins include lying, extortion, and false swearing. God required His people to bring a guilt or trespass offering for intentional sins. These willful sins are different from sinning "with a high hand."[38] The phrase "with a high hand" pictures a person lifting his fist in rebellion and defying God as he does wrong. God provided no sacrifice for such rebellion in the Old Testament. The person who sinned with a high hand was to be cut off from God's people and killed.[39]

You're probably wondering why God made it so complicated. In one way God made it very simple: Leviticus teaches us that any violation of God's word is sin, and a blood sacrifice for atonement is required for us to be forgiven and to have fellowship with our holy God. Jesus had to die to provide atonement for all of our sins, whether they were intentional or unintentional. On the other hand, Leviticus also teaches us through the sacrificial system that God recognizes the difference between willful sin, unintentional sin, and infirmities, and He wants us to know the difference too.

---

36 Exodus 22:5-6.
37 Leviticus 16; see also Hebrews 9:7.
38 **Numbers 15:30** "But the person who does *anything* presumptuously [with a high hand], *whether he is* native-born or a stranger, that one brings reproach on the LORD, and he shall be cut off from among his people."
39 In the New Testament we learn that because of Jesus' sacrifice God will forgive any kind of sin, including sins of a high hand. The only sin God will not forgive is blasphemy against the Holy Spirit (see Mat. 12:31; Mark 3:29). Blasphemy against the Holy Spirit is deliberately attributing to the devil what you know is the work of the Holy Spirit. Jesus warned the Pharisees that they were in danger of this eternal sin when they accused Him of casting out demons by the power of the devil. They knew or should have known that He was casting out demons by the power of the Holy Spirit.

Sin and Salvation in the New Testament

God's purpose in sending His Son into the world was to destroy the works of the devil.[40] That's why His name is Jesus: He came to save us from our sins—not just our acts of sin, or even from the principle of sin, but also from the *effects* of sin including death.[41] God's plan is to do away with sin comprehensively so we can be holy and again have loving fellowship with our holy God forever.

However, God doesn't save us from *all* sin and its effects all at once. The plan of salvation unfolds in stages. When we are saved, the record of our sin is removed,[42] we are freed from sin's control over us,[43] we are cleansed from all our past acts of sin, and as long as we walk in the light we are cleansed from any unintentional sins we might commit.[44] In entire sanctification God deals with the principle of sin which makes us self-centered and inclined to do evil.[45] Throughout the course of our walk with God, He is in the process of removing the effects of sin on our minds and hearts and renewing us in the image of His Son. This is called progressive sanctification. In glorification, which takes place when we die (or when Jesus returns), we are perfected in the image of Christ. The final stage is salvation from sin's effects by the resurrection of our physical bodies to immortality.

> **The plan of salvation unfolds in stages.**

---

40 **1 John 3:8** "He who sins is of the devil, for the devil has sinned from the beginning. For this purpose the Son of God was manifested, that He might destroy the works of the devil."
41 **Matthew 1:21** "And she will bring forth a Son, and you shall call His name Jesus, for He will save His people from their sins." The name "Jesus" means "The LORD saves."
42 **Romans 4:7-8** "Blessed *are those* whose lawless deeds are forgiven, And whose sins are covered; Blessed *is the* man to whom the LORD shall not impute sin."
43 **Romans 6:6-7** "Knowing this, that our old man was crucified with *Him,* that the body of sin might be done away with, that we should no longer be slaves of sin. For he who has died has been freed from sin."
44 **1 John 1:7** "But if we walk in the light as He is in the light, we have fellowship with one another, and the blood of Jesus Christ His Son cleanses us from all sin." Of course, when we realize that we have committed an unintentional sin, we must repent of it and ask God's forgiveness.
45 For further discussion of entire sanctification, see chapters 11 & 12.

Freedom from Sin

The wonderful message of Scripture is that we can be free from sin and live holy lives because of Christ. We do not have to sin. We are free from bondage to sin! In fact, John says it is impossible for a person who is right with God to live in sin.[46] In Christ we have the power to live free from all willful sin.

> **We do not have to sin.**

Freedom from sin is one of the most important themes of God's word and plays a central role in Wesleyan-Arminian theology. Other theological systems, such as Calvinism, have concluded that believers are not able to keep God's law perfectly, and as a result cannot help but sin every day in word, thought, and deed.[47]

As we have already noted, when the New Testament talks about freedom from sin or not living in sin, it is always referring to freedom from intentional or willful sin. There are several ways we know this, but 1 John is probably the book that makes this the clearest. John tells us that we must walk in the light to have fellowship with God.[48] If we are walking in the light, we are not intentionally doing anything we know is wrong. John also says that those who abide in Christ do not practice sin.[49] Putting these

---

[46] **1 John 3:9** "Whoever has been born of God does not sin, for His seed remains in him; and he cannot [continue in] sin, because he has been born of God." The way John worded this verse indicates that he meant that someone who is born of God cannot *continue* to practice sin. He did not mean it is impossible for a Christian to sin.

[47] The Westminster Shorter Catechism, question 82 reads, "Is any man able perfectly to keep the commandments of God? A. No mere man [i.e., human] since the fall is able in this life perfectly to keep the commandments of God, but doth daily break them in thought, word, and deed (Gen. 6:5; Gen. 8:21; Rom. 3:9-21; James 3:2-13)." When this statement from the Westminster catechism is quoted to support the belief that we all sin daily, the person quoting it normally means we all sin willfully every day. This conclusion contradicts what the New Testament teaches about the believer's freedom from willful sin.

[48] **1 John 1:7** "But if we walk in the light as He is in the light, we have fellowship with one another, and the blood of Jesus Christ His Son cleanses us from all sin."

[49] **1 John 3:6** "Whoever abides in Him does not [practice] sin. Whoever [practices] sin has neither seen Him nor known Him."

two statements together, we can see that Christians do not practice willful sin.

The promise of 1 John 1:7 is that Jesus' blood cleanses from all sin. Wesleyan-Arminian theologians have concluded that this includes sins of ignorance. In other words, as long as you are walking in all the light you have, God does not hold any involuntary or ignorant sins you commit against you. One of the reasons for this is that Jesus is our sin offering. His sacrifice on the cross provides atonement for all our unintentional sins, just like the sin offering did on the Day of Atonement in the Old Testament.[50]

You may wonder, "If God doesn't hold unintentional sins against us when we're walking in the light, why call them 'sin'?" There are several reasons we should call unintentional violations of God's word "sin." (1) God calls them sin. (2) They are offenses against God's holiness. (3) They required the sacrifice of Jesus' life on the cross to propitiate God's wrath against us and remove our guilt. (4) God requires us to repent and make restitution when we realize we have violated His word unintentionally. (5) We will reap the temporal consequences of our wrong doing. God doesn't stop the law of sowing and reaping for unintentional sins. This highlights the seriousness of unintentional sins. They will not keep us out of heaven, but they may cause much damage in our interpersonal relationships, and in the church, and even hinder sinners from being saved. This is why we should pray David's prayer in Psalm 19:13, "Cleanse me from secret *faults*."

As we grow in spiritual maturity, we should learn how to avoid stumbling.[51] If we do stumble, we should immediately ask

---

50 **Hebrews 9:7, 11-12** "But into the second part the high priest *went* alone once a year, not without blood, which he offered for himself and *for* the people's sins *committed* in ignorance . . . . But Christ came *as* High Priest of the good things to come, with the greater and more perfect tabernacle not made with hands, that is, not of this creation. Not with the blood of goats and calves, but with His own blood He entered the Most Holy Place once for all, having obtained eternal redemption."
51 Matthew 5:29-30; 2 Peter 1:10.

forgiveness and purpose by God's grace to avoid erring in that way again.

Praise the Lord that He has enabled us to live above willful sin and has provided an automatic cleansing for any unintentional sins through the blood of Jesus!

Some Practical Issues

➡ Do Christians sin willfully "every day in word, thought, and deed"?

The Bible's answer is a resounding "God forbid!"[52] In stark contrast to our bondage as sinners, when we trust in Christ we are freed from sin's control over us.[53] As Paul says, "But now having been set free from sin, and having become slaves of God, you have your fruit to holiness, and the end, everlasting life."[54] John wrote his epistle for the very purpose of telling us that we should not ever sin.[55] As believers, we do not practice willful sin, because we love God and want to do what pleases Him.[56]

In addition to freedom from sin's control, 1 Cor. 10:13 promises that God never allows a Christian to be tempted beyond his capacity to resist the temptation through God's grace. Therefore, *no Christian ever has to sin willfully*. If a Christian does sin willfully when tempted, it is because he did not make use of God's grace. If we commit a willful sin, it damages our relationship with God, and if we refuse to confess and repent of it, it will separate us from God.

---

52 **Romans 6:1-2** "What shall we say then? Shall we continue in sin, that grace may abound? God forbid! How shall we, who died to sin, live any longer therein?" (KJV).
53 **Romans 6:6-7** "Knowing this, that our old man was crucified with *Him,* that the body of sin might be done away with, that we should no longer be slaves of sin. For he who has died has been freed from sin."
54 Romans 6:22.
55 **1 John 2:1** "My little children, these things I write to you, so that you may not sin. And if anyone sins, we have an Advocate with the Father, Jesus Christ the righteous."
56 **1 John 3:6** "Whoever abides in Him does not sin. Whoever sins has neither seen Him nor known Him."

1 John 3:8 "He who sins is of the devil, for the devil has sinned from the beginning. For this purpose the Son of God was manifested, that He might destroy the works of the devil."

➡ What does it mean to live above willful sin?

It does not mean that a Christian cannot be tempted. There is no level of Christlikeness or spiritual maturity that frees us from temptation, for Christ Himself was tempted (Mat. 4). Therefore, it also does not mean that a Christian cannot sin willfully. No orthodox theologian, Wesleyan or otherwise, has ever claimed that we can reach a level where we are unable to sin willfully. The writer of Hebrews, in fact, explicitly urges us to exhort one another daily to beware of the deceitfulness of sin.[57] We are still capable of willful sin.[58]

It does mean that Christians do not have to sin willfully. Stated positively, at every decision point in life a Christian can, because of God's grace, choose to do right. It means that Christians can live lives characterized by obedience to all the truth of God's word that they know. We **can** walk in the light as He is in the light.[59] We **can** live holy, just, and blameless lives.[60]

> **At every decision point a Christian can choose to do right.**

The Bible directly affirms that Zacharias and Elizabeth lived above willful sin.[61] Paul testifies that this is the way he lived his life: "For our confidence is this: the testimony of our conscience, that in holiness and godly sincerity, not in fleshly wisdom but in the grace of God, we have conducted ourselves in the world, and especially toward you."[62]

---

57 **Hebrews 3:13** "But exhort one another daily, while it is called 'Today,' lest any of you be hardened through the deceitfulness of sin."
58 **Hebrews 10:26** "For if we sin willfully after we have received the knowledge of the truth, there no longer remains a sacrifice for sins."
59 **1 John 1:7** "But if we walk in the light as He is in the light, we have fellowship with one another, and the blood of Jesus Christ His Son cleanses us from all sin."
60 **1 John 2:10** "He who loves his brother abides in the light, and there is no cause for stumbling in him."
61 **Luke 1:6** "And they were both righteous before God, walking in all the commandments and ordinances of the Lord blameless."
62 2 Corinthians 1:12 (NASB).

➡ How does a Christian live above willful sin?

The shortest answer is "By grace." The Bible gives us more specific directions than this. However, it is crucial to realize that a Christian can live above willful sin *only by total dependence upon God's grace.* Living above willful sin is the result of God's grace enabling us (1) to love God totally, for love keeps His commands; (2) to walk in the Spirit, for "If you are walking in the Spirit, you will never fulfill the lusts of the flesh;"[63] (3) to not make provision for the lusts of the flesh;[64] (4) to resist the devil's temptations;[65] (5) to flee youthful lusts;[66] and (6) to pursue "righteousness, faith, love and peace, with those who call on the Lord from a pure heart."[67]

➡ As a Christian, what am I supposed to do if I do sin willfully?

If we do sin, 1 John 2:1 says Jesus is our advocate when we confess and repent of our sin. An advocate is someone who helps another person by pleading his case. When we repent, Jesus pleads our case with the Father. Although the Scripture does not tell us exactly how Jesus pleads our case, He probably says something like, "Father, I bore your wrath on the cross for their sin. They have repented and are asking forgiveness. Please forgive them for my sake." And the Father, true to His word, is "faithful and just to forgive us our sins and to cleanse us from all unrighteousness."[68]

---

63 **Galatians 5:16** "I say then: Walk in the Spirit, and you shall not fulfill the lust of the flesh." The logical conclusion from this verse is any time you fulfill the lusts of the flesh, it must be because you are not walking in the Spirit.
64 **Romans 13:14** "But put on the Lord Jesus Christ, and make no provision for the flesh, to *fulfill its* lusts."
65 **James 4:7** "Therefore submit to God. Resist the devil and he will flee from you."
66 **2 Timothy 2:22a** "Flee also youthful lusts . . . ."
67 **2 Timothy 2:22b** "... but pursue righteousness, faith, love, peace with those who call on the Lord out of a pure heart."
68 **1 John 1:9.** For quotations from John Wesley, Daniel Steele, and other holiness writers who make the same point, see W. T. Purkiser, *Interpreting Christian Holiness* (Kansas City: Beacon Hill, 1971), 25-29.

→ What happens to a person who refuses to repent of willful sin?

If that person has never been saved, he will ultimately be separated from God forever in the Lake of Fire. If a person who has known Christ refuses to repent of willful sin, he is rejecting his relationship with Christ and thereby forfeiting eternal life. Paul tells us in Romans 11:20 that believers are united to Christ through faith. If a person turns away from obedient faith in Christ, he will be cut out of Christ.[69] If he persists in his disobedient unbelief, he too will ultimately be separated from God forever in the Lake of Fire. God promises eternal security to all those who by grace are living out their faith in Christ through obedience to the will of God.[70] He promises no security to anyone whose faith is not lived out in obedience to God's will.[71]

I Believe . . .

We are born with corruption affecting every part of our being. This corruption manifests itself in self-centeredness and inclines us to sin. Any violation of God's word is a sin against God and requires the cleansing of Christ's blood. All Christians have been freed from sin's control and can live above willful sin by God's grace. The effects of sin on our minds are removed gradually by the Spirit through the renewing of the Word of God. All the effects of sin on us will be removed when we are glorified and are fully like Christ.

---

[69] **Romans 11:21-23** "For if God did not spare the natural branches, He may not spare you either. Therefore consider the goodness and severity of God: on those who fell, severity; but toward you, goodness, if you continue in His goodness. Otherwise you also will be cut off. And they also, if they do not continue in unbelief, will be grafted in, for God is able to graft them in again."

[70] **1 Peter 1:5** "[We] are kept by the power of God through faith for salvation ready to be revealed in the last time."

[71] **1 John 2:4** "He who says, 'I know Him,' and does not keep His commandments, is a liar, and the truth is not in him."

Questions for Study

1. What is the root of every problem in the world?
2. What does the word sin mean?
3. Scripture uses the word sin in two different ways. What are they?
4. What are the primary terms the Bible uses for the principle of sin?
5. What is the principle of sin or the law of sin?
6. What is depravity?
7. What does the term **total depravity** mean?
8. What is the classic passage that describes the extent of total depravity?
9. In addition to our sinning with our actions, in what two other areas can we sin?
10. What is one of the primary reasons God put Leviticus in the Bible?
11. What are the three crucial truths Leviticus teaches us about acts of sin?
12. What are the two kinds of sinful acts that Leviticus distinguishes?
13. What is unintentional sin?
14. What is intentional sin?
15. How do we know that human infirmities are not sin?
16. What are the five major stages in the unfolding of the plan of salvation?
17. What are five reasons why unintentional violations of God's word are called sins?
18. What should a person do if he realizes he has sinned unintentionally?

19. What verse in the New Testament promises us that God will never let us be tempted beyond our capacity to resist through His grace?

Recommended Reading

Forlines, F. Leroy. *The Quest for Truth: Answering Life's Inescapable Questions*. Nashville: Randall House, 2000. See especially Appendix 1: "Sins of Ignorance and Presumptuous Sins in the Old and New Testaments," 467-488.

Kinghorn, Kenneth. "Biblical Concepts of Sin," *Wesleyan Theological Journal* 1, 1966; online at http://wesley.nnu.edu/wesleyan_theology/theojrnl/01-05/01-3.htm>.

Wesley, John. "On Sin in Believers," in *The Complete Works of Wesley*. Vol. 5, Sermon 13.

_____, "The Doctrine of Original Sin," in *The Complete Works of Wesley*. Vol. 9

_____, "Plain Account Of Christian Perfection," in *The Complete Works of Wesley*. Vol. 11. See especially his discussion of sin under the question, "If they live without sin, does this not exclude the necessity of a mediator?"

Wilcox, Leslie. *Profiles in Wesleyan Theology*. Salem, OH: Schmul Publishing, 1985. See Chapter 7: "Origin and Nature of Sin," 141-170.

6

The Real Jesus

I have never forgotten the unusual conversation that I once had with a hitchhiker. We had not traveled very long together when I realized my rider was in some kind of a cult. He said that he would "come to power" in about 10 years and would end up being responsible for annihilating thousands, maybe millions of people. He went on and on, both amusing me and perturbing me. Finally, I turned to him and said, "So, who are you, anyway?" He looked me in the eye, paused, then said, "I am he, the third Son of the Father, the Prince of Peace!"

Though this man probably hasn't gained much of a following, the Bible does predict that in the last days, false Christs and false prophets would come and deceive many. A lot of people these days are putting their faith in false or imaginary Christs who cannot save them. You might meet two of these false Christs —introduced to you by the Mormons and the Jehovah's Witnesses.

The Mormons' Jesus

If a Mormon ever knocks on your door, he will bring a Jesus who is the spirit-brother of Lucifer. This Jesus is one of the billions of spirit-babies that our "Heavenly Father" and our "Heavenly Mother" brought into this universe. According to the Mormons, when Jesus lived on earth, he had several wives, one of whom was Mary Magdalene. After his death and resurrection, he came to America to preach to the Indians.

The Jehovah's Witnesses' Jesus

The Jehovah's Witnesses will tell you that Jesus is Michael the Archangel, the first created being, who became a man and died on a stake instead of a cross. He was raised as a spirit-creature, becoming Michael the Archangel again, while his body was dissolved into gases.

The Real Jesus

You can probably see that these cultists have a false Jesus, but can you describe the true, biblical Jesus? A lot of Americans can't. A recent survey showed that though 80% of Americans would call Jesus the Son of God, only 40% believed that He was God, and only 40% believed He was sinless. This shows that millions of people have a mental concept of a false Christ, one who cannot save them.

It is important for you to be certain of your beliefs about Jesus so that you are not deceived, and so you can introduce Him to others.

So what *do* we believe concerning Jesus? Our basic beliefs about Jesus could be divided into three categories, connected to three special days that we celebrate.

We Celebrate Christmas because of the Incarnation

> **While Jesus was a baby, His mother Mary held and rocked the One who had created her.**

When I was very young, I was puzzled by a Christmas song that I heard several times on the radio. One phrase was sung over and over: "The birds and Mary had a baby boy. The birds and Mary had a baby boy...." At least that's what I thought the song said. Actually, the words were, "The *virgin* Mary had a baby boy."

Christmas celebrates the birth of Jesus to a virgin mother,[1] for Jesus was conceived by the Holy Spirit.[2] Though Jesus was human because He was born of a woman, He was also God Himself, the Creator of the world He entered. This is amazing but true: while Jesus was a baby, His mother Mary held and rocked the One who had created her.

God's nature and human nature had come together in the person of Jesus. This is called the *incarnation*, which means God taking on human flesh, becoming a man.

Even Jesus' name helps us understand who He is and why He became incarnate. The name Jesus means "The LORD saves." He was given that name because He would "save His people from their sins."[3] Jesus was the only One who could be our Savior because He is the only person in the universe both man and God.

➡ Jesus is a Man.

It is not hard to recognize the Jesus of the New Testament as truly human. He was conceived in a mother's womb, grew up, learned, and developed as a person.[4] He got tired, slept, was tempted, and did about everything else that a human would do, except sin. He even died. He truly identified with the human race by becoming one of us.[5]

If Jesus were not a man, He could not have suffered and died. If Jesus were not man, His righteous life could not take the place of our sinful life; He could not have been our substitute. If He were not a man, Jesus would not qualify to be our priest who pro-

---

[1] **Luke 1:34** "Then Mary said to the angel, 'How can this [pregnancy] be, since I do not know a man?'"
[2] **Luke 1:35** "And the angel answered and said to her, 'The Holy Spirit will come upon you, and the power of the Highest will overshadow you; therefore, also, that Holy One who is to be born will be called the Son of God.'"
[3] Matthew 1:21.
[4] **Luke 2:52** "And Jesus increased in wisdom and stature, and in favor with God and men."
[5] **John 1:14** "And the Word became flesh and dwelt among us, and we beheld His glory, the glory as of the only begotten of the Father, full of grace and truth."

vided an eternal salvation.[6] The humanity of Jesus is an essential part of the gospel.[7]

➡ Jesus is God.

The Jesus of the Bible is not simply a human, however. He is also the one infinite (limitless) God of the universe. Jesus makes this claim Himself. He said, "I and my Father are One."[8] When He said this, the Jews started to stone Him because they understood Him to be saying that He was equal to God. Did Jesus tell them, "No, you misunderstood Me. I am not really God!"? No, Jesus accepted their interpretation of His words. He taught that He was equal to God the Father.

> He taught that He was equal to God the Father.

When Jesus said, "Before Abraham was, I AM,"[9] He was claiming to be the I AM of Exodus 3:14, the self-existent God of the universe.[10] The Jews tried to stone Him for this claim as well.[11]

He performed divine acts while on earth.

Not only did Jesus make divine claims, but He also performed divine acts while He was on the earth. He gave eternal life.[12] He forgave sins.[13] These are things that only God can do.

---

6 **Hebrews 10:5-7** "Therefore when He came into the world, He said: 'Sacrifice and offering You did not desire, but a body You have prepared for Me. In burnt offerings and sacrifices for sin You had no pleasure.' Then I said, 'Behold, I have come—in the volume of the book it is written of Me—to do Your will, O God.'" See also 5:7-9 and 4:15.
7 **1 John 5:1** "Whoever believes that Jesus is the Christ is born of God, and everyone who loves Him who begot also loves him who is begotten of Him."
8 John 10:30.
9 John 8:58.
10 **Exodus 3:14** "And God said to Moses, 'I AM WHO I AM.' And He said, 'Thus you shall say to the children of Israel, "I AM has sent me to you."'"
11 John 8:59.
12 **John 10:28** "And I give them eternal life, and they shall never perish; neither shall anyone snatch them out of My hand."
13 **Mark 2:10** "But that you may know that the Son of Man has power on earth to forgive sins—He said to the paralytic, 'I say to you, arise, take up your bed, and go your way to your house.'"

When Jesus forgave the sins of the paralytic, He healed the man to prove that He had "power on earth to forgive sins."[14] One action was proof of the other, making it clear that Jesus had not performed the miracle of healing as simply a prophet anointed by God. Jesus had the divine authority both to forgive and to heal.

He also resurrected Lazarus after saying, "I am the Resurrection and the Life."[15] This was another divine action accompanied by a divine claim. Only God can rightfully claim to *be* the "Resurrection" because it is only the power of God that can raise anyone from the dead. Jesus claimed to be this "Life-giver" and then gave Lazarus life, showing that He was who He claimed to be.[16]

When Jesus performed His miracles, He "manifested His glory,"[17] the "glory as of the only begotten of the Father, full of grace and truth."[18] These miracles were demonstrations of God the Son's glorious power, proving He was divine.

He is Creator and Sustainer.

According to the Apostles John and Paul, Jesus created everything[19] and holds everything together.[20] Surely this could not be said of anyone but God.

It is important to know that Jesus is God.

If Jesus were not God, then His sacrificial death would not be of infinite value—enough for forgiveness of the sins of the world. If He were not God, He would not have the power to save us, but because He is God, He is the way, the truth, and the life.

---

14 Mark 2:10-12.
15 John 11:25.
16 In this event, Jesus clearly distinguished Himself from other prophets and the apostles who raised people from the dead by the power of God. None of these claimed to have the power in and of themselves to do the work. They were simply instruments of God. In John 5:21, Jesus said that He raises the dead just as the Father raises the dead.
17 John 2:11.
18 John 1:14.
19 **John 1:3** "All things were made through Him, and without Him nothing was made that was made."
20 **Colossians 1:17** "And He is before all things, and in Him all things consist."

If we fail to see Jesus as God, we will not honor Him as God, which is something Jesus says we must do. He said that "all should honor the Son, just as they honor the Father."[21] We can't be saved if we don't honor both the Father and the Son as God.

Christianity is based not only on the teachings and actions of Jesus, but on the unique person of Jesus. He is not just the teacher of the message of salvation. He is Himself the Savior, and only He —the God-man—could have been the Savior.

➡ Jesus is One Person.

Though Jesus has all of the nature of God and all of the nature of man, He is not two persons combined. The two natures form one person in Him, in perfect harmony. Jesus is the one God-man, and every action of Jesus has to be understood in light of His full humanity and full deity.

The church has always taught that the two natures in Jesus cannot be separated from one another, yet they are not mixed in a way that causes either nature to lose its characteristics.[22]

It may be helpful to compare the nature of Jesus to the nature of the Holy Scriptures. Like Jesus, the Bible is fully divine and fully human. Being a human book, it has the characteristics of any other human book, except that it is without mistake. Being divine, it consistently exhibits divine characteristics that no other book could. In the same way, Jesus consistently exhibits both human and divine qualities. The fact that the Bible shows divine characteristics does not make it any less of a human book. Likewise, the fact that Jesus operates in His deity doesn't make Him any less human. And the fact that Christ operates in His humanity doesn't make Him any less divine.

> **Jesus is not just the teacher of the message of salvation.**

---

21 John 5:23.
22 The Chalcedonian Creed (A.D. 451) says that the two natures of Christ are unchanging, indivisible, inseparable, and unconfused.

We Celebrate Good Friday because of the Atonement[23]

Good Friday is the day that Jesus was crucified. On this dreadful and wonderful day, Jesus took our sins to the cross. He died as a sacrifice for our sins so that we can be forgiven.

➡ A sacrifice was necessary.

A sacrifice had to be made in order for God to forgive us and still be just and holy. This principle was taught in the Old Testament by the sacrifices God said must be offered.[24] If God simply forgave sin without a basis, it would indicate that He is not just and that sin is not very serious. But nobody could look at Jesus' death by crucifixion and say that sin is not serious. His sacrifice provided the basis for our forgiveness.

➡ Only Jesus could be a sufficient sacrifice.

The justice of God and the seriousness of sin required a greater sacrifice than any created thing could be.[25] We have sinned against an infinite God, which brings upon us infinite guilt. That is why only Jesus could be the sacrifice. He was qualified because He was God, and because He was man. Because He was God, He was sinless, and His sacrifice had infinite value. Because He was man, He could represent us and die in our place.

> **He grasped God's hand on one side and man's hand on the other.**

➡ Jesus brought God and man together.

Jesus came to reconcile two separated parties—God and man. As the mediator, Jesus had to represent both parties at the same time. As God, He represented God to man. As man, He represented man to God. By fully representing both sides, Jesus brought

---

23 *To atone* means to provide an adequate basis for forgiveness so that sins can be taken away. It results in *at-one-ment*, or reconciliation with God.
24 **Hebrews 9:22** "And according to the law almost all things are purged with blood, and without shedding of blood there is no remission."
25 **Hebrews 10:4** "For it is not possible that the blood of bulls and goats could take away sins."

man and God together. It's as though He grasped God's hand on one side and man's hand on the other and pulled us back together. He did what each side had to do to bring about reconciliation.

We Celebrate Easter because of the Resurrection

A lot of people only understand Easter as the time of the Easter bunny. Once a year, this legendary rabbit mysteriously lays brightly-colored eggs, a symbol of springtime and new life. While I don't honor the Easter bunny or Easter eggs, I am not sure that the association of Easter eggs with Easter is completely artificial, for Easter *does* have a lot to say about new life. Jesus rose from the grave on Easter morning, the third day after He was crucified. He showed that He had power over sin, death, and the devil. He not only took our death, but conquered it with life. Because He was victorious, we can be too!

➡ **Jesus arose bodily.**

Jesus once said to the Jews, "Destroy this temple, and in three days I will raise it up." Though the Jews thought He was referring to the temple that Herod built, John's Gospel explains that Jesus was actually referring to His body.[26] All the Gospels record the fact that Jesus' tomb was empty three days after He was buried in it. The tomb was empty because the body itself had been raised. Jesus showed Himself to the disciples after His resurrection, saying, "Handle me, and see, for a spirit does not have flesh and bones as you see I have."[27] He was proving that He had literally, physically risen from the dead.

Jesus' bodily resurrection demonstrated His total victory over sin and death.[28]

---

[26] John 2:19-21.
[27] Luke 24:39.
[28] **Colossians 2:14-15** "[Jesus] wiped out the handwriting of requirements that was against us, which was contrary to us. And He has taken it out of the way, having nailed it to the cross. Having disarmed principalities and powers, He made a public spectacle of them, triumphing over them in it."

Jesus' bodily resurrection proved that He was who He claimed to be. Thus it also proved the gospel. People who deny that Jesus literally, bodily rose from the dead also deny the gospel. [29]

Jesus' resurrection gives us the assurance that we will also be raised from the dead. Jesus promised that He would raise the dead, but that would be unbelievable unless He Himself arose.[30] We will be raised to have bodies like Jesus' glorified body.[31]

➡ **Jesus is still human.**

The resurrection shows us that the incarnation is permanent. Jesus will always be human as well as divine. God has added human nature to His own nature for eternity, in order to restore His creatures to a love relationship with Himself. Jesus, still the God-man, now intercedes for us with the Father,[32] and will someday return to take us to heaven.[33]

We Yield to Jesus because of Who He Is and What He Did

If you accept the truths we just shared about Jesus, but haven't yet yielded to His rightful claim on your life, I would encourage you to pray this prayer sincerely:

Father, I thank you for loving me enough to send your Son Jesus into the world for my sake. I believe that Jesus is the sinless God-man who died and rose again so I could be forgiven for my sins and be restored to a relationship with you. I am very sorry for all the sins I have committed. I know my

---

29 **1 Corinthians 15:17** "And if Christ is not risen, your faith is futile; you are still in your sins."
30 **John 5:28-29** "Do not marvel at this; for the hour is coming in which all who are in the graves will hear His voice and come forth—those who have done good, to the resurrection of life, and those who have done evil, to the resurrection of condemnation."
31 **1 John 3:2** ". . . but we know that when He is revealed, we shall be like Him, for we shall see Him as He is. " **Philippians 3:21** "Who will transform our lowly body that it may be conformed to His glorious body . . . ."
32 **Romans 8:34** "Who *is* he who condemns? *It is* Christ who died, and furthermore is also risen, who is even at the right hand of God, who also makes intercession for us."
33 **1 Thessalonians 4:16-17** "For the Lord Himself will descend from heaven with a shout, with the voice of an archangel, and with the trumpet of God. And the dead in Christ will rise first. Then we who are alive *and* remain shall be caught up together with them in the clouds to meet the Lord in the air. And thus we shall always be with the Lord."

sins nailed Jesus to the cross. *So right now I turn away from everything I know is wrong, and I receive Jesus into my heart and life as my Lord and Savior. Lead me from now on. I am going to live for you forever! Thank you for forgiving me. I love you. Amen.*

I Believe . . .

The sinless life, sacrificial death, and triumphant resurrection of the God-man, Jesus Christ, were all for the sake of offering salvation to every person. The repenting, believing sinner receives forgiveness and is restored to a relationship with God, on the basis of Christ's atonement.

Questions for Study

1. What does it mean that Jesus is an incarnation?
2. Why is it important that Jesus is a man?
3. What is some scriptural evidence that Jesus is God?
4. Why is it important that Jesus is God?
5. Why did Jesus die?
6. What is the significance of Jesus' resurrection?

Recommended Reading

Strobel, Lee. *The Case for Christ.* Grand Rapids: Zondervan, 1998.

Zacharias, Ravi. *Jesus Among Other Gods.* Nashville: Word Publishing, 2000.

7

The Holy Spirit

My brother Dave was the area supervisor of several gas stations. Every day he visited each of his stores. One morning he left early and started for the farthest store on his route. Dave was feeling depressed, and with no one in the car with him, he had few distractions from his feelings. The emptiness of his life troubled him. The road trip was getting miserable. Then suddenly, he heard a voice, an audible voice! Someone in that car said, "Jesus loves you!" In shock, my brother turned to his right. He saw no one. *Who was that?! Was it God?* "Forgive me!" Dave cried out. Then something happened in his heart. God gave him the assurance right then that he was a new creature in Christ. Discovering that he no longer wanted the cigarettes in his front pocket, Dave threw them onto the car floor to be thrown away when he reached his destination. When he got home that night, he poured out the alcohol from the bar in his basement. He gathered his family around the dining room table, and told them that things would be different in their home. And they were. That was almost twenty years ago, and my brother is still a strong Christian.

Now my question to you is: Who spoke to my brother going down the highway? Was it an angel? Was it Jesus? Was it Dave's imagination? I believe the voice Dave heard that morning was the voice of the Holy Spirit. Why does He speak? He speaks (though usually not audibly) because He is a Person, because He is God, and because His work is to bring each of us into a delightful, personal relationship with Jesus.

The Holy Spirit Is a Person.

Some people don't think the Holy Spirit can speak because they think of the Holy Spirit as an impersonal force, or simply a presence. For instance, a Jehovah's Witness will say something like this:

> "The holy spirit is not a person and it is not a part of a Trinity. The holy spirit is God's active force that he uses to accomplish his will. . . . To a certain extent, it can be likened to electricity."[1]

The Jehovah's Witness sees the Holy Spirit as an impersonal force.

Maybe you have trouble thinking of the Holy Spirit as a real person. After all, He doesn't have a physical body like Jesus does. But He is a person who has eternally lived in a personal love relationship with God the Father and God the Son. And now He invites each of us to participate in that dynamic love relationship.

◆ Biblical Proof that the Holy Spirit Is a Person

A real person has the attributes of personality, which include mind, will, and emotions. Does the Holy Spirit have a will? He distributes spiritual gifts to Christians, "as He wills."[2] Does the Holy Spirit have a mind? He "searches . . . the deep things of God" and knows them.[3] Does the Holy Spirit have emotions? We are told to "grieve not the Holy Spirit."[4] If the Holy Spirit can be grieved, then He has emotions. Because the Holy Spirit has a mind, a will, and emotions, we know that He is a Person.[5]

A real person also has the capacity to have relationships with others. That's the primary reason we have mind, will, and emotions. According to Philippians 2:1, the Spirit is able to have fel-

---

1 *Should You Believe in the Trinity?* New York: The Watchtower Bible and Tract Soc., 1989.
2 **1 Corinthians 12:11** "But one and the same Spirit works all these things, distributing to each one individually as He wills."
3 **1 Corinthians 2:10** "But God has revealed them to us through His Spirit. For the Spirit searches all things, yes, the deep things of God."
4 Ephesians 4:30.
5 Here are other passages that describe the Holy Spirit's doing something that only a person could do: Acts 16:6, Acts 8:28, Matthew 10:16-20, and Romans 8:26.

lowship with us.[6] According to 2 Corinthians 13:14, the Holy Spirit can have communion with us.[7] One who is able to commune and to have fellowship is capable of personal relationships. Therefore the Holy Spirit is a person.

◆ What This Means for You

Understand that the Holy Spirit is a real Person, not just a force or a presence or a power. You must recognize Him as a Person. He can talk to you.[8] He is praying for you,[9] just as Christ is praying for you. He will teach you what you need to know. He will guide you in your decisions. He tells you that you are a child of God.[10] He will personally clean up the "rooms" of your innermost being when you let Him. You can submit to His voice or reject His voice. If you disobey His voice, He will be grieved. If you persist in your disobedience, you will grieve Him out of your life. Respecting the Holy Spirit as a person is necessary for your relationship with Him.

◆ Listening to the Spirit

Take time to listen for the Spirit. Don't wait for an audible voice—He rarely speaks audibly—but listen as He speaks through God's word. Learn to understand what many call "the prompts" and "the checks" of the Spirit. You will experience these because the Spirit, as a divine Person, has taken a personal interest in you. Have you ever thanked Him for that?

The Holy Spirit Is God.

The Holy Spirit is the all-knowing, all-seeing, everywhere-present God. Acts 5:3-4 teaches us that the Holy Spirit is

---

6 "Therefore if *there is* any consolation in Christ, if any comfort of love, if any fellowship of the Spirit . . . ."
6 "The grace of the Lord Jesus Christ, and the love of God, and the communion of the Holy Spirit *be* with you all."
8 **Acts 8:29** "Then the Spirit said to Philip, 'Go near and overtake this chariot.'"
9 **Romans 8:26** "For we do not know what we should pray for as we ought, but the Spirit Himself makes intercession for us with groanings which cannot be uttered."
10 **Romans 8:15-16** "For you did not receive the spirit of bondage again to fear, but you received the Spirit of adoption by whom we cry out, 'Abba, Father.' The Spirit Himself bears witness with our spirit that we are children of God."

God. Remember the story of Ananias and Sapphira? Before Ananias was struck dead, Peter told him, "Why has Satan filled your heart to lie to the Holy Spirit? . . . You have not lied to men; but to God." From this event we can see that lying to the Holy Spirit is the same as lying to God; therefore, the Holy Spirit is God.

There is more Scriptural evidence that the Holy Spirit is God. We see from the Bible that:

The words of God are the words the Holy Spirit inspired;[11]

We are the temple of God because the Spirit indwells us;[12]

The one born of the Spirit is said to be born of God;[13]

The Holy Spirit is God Himself, the third Person of the divine Trinity. Why is it so important to believe in the deity and personhood of the Holy Spirit? It is crucial because you cannot give Him the honor and respect that He deserves if you don't consider Him a divine Person. In fact, it is doubtful that someone can be saved while he denies the personhood and deity of the One who tries to draw him to salvation.

The Holy Spirit Is Distinct from the Father and the Son.

One person I talked to declared, "The Holy Spirit is Jesus." Some people think that the Holy Spirit is actually the same Person as the Father and the Son. But the Scriptures clearly teach a distinction between the Persons of the Trinity. For example, again and again in John 14-16, Jesus referred to a Helper ("Comforter" in the KJV) that He would send when He went back to the Father.[14] This Helper would guide the disciples and teach

---

11 **2 Timothy 3:16** "All Scripture is given by inspiration of God, and is profitable for doctrine, for reproof, for correction, for instruction in righteousness."
12 **1 Corinthians 6:19** "Or do you not know that your body is the temple of the Holy Spirit, who is in you, whom ye have from God, and you are not your own?"
13 **John 3:5-8.** In Jesus' conversation with Nicodemus, He said that it is necessary to "be born of water and the Spirit." Further He said, "You must be born again." Then He referred to the one who has been born again as "born of the Spirit."
14 **John 15:26** "But when the Helper comes, whom I shall send to you from the Father, the Spirit of truth who proceeds from the Father, He will testify of Me.

them.[15] If Jesus and the Holy Spirit were one and the same Person, Jesus' reference to the Holy Spirit as *another* Helper would not make sense. Jesus must have been referring to *another* Person distinct from Himself.

Look at the story of Jesus' baptism.[16] Here the Son is baptized, a voice from Heaven says, "This is my beloved Son," and the Holy Spirit, like a dove, rests upon Jesus. All of this occurs simultaneously. All of the three members of the Trinity are seen here at the same time, obviously distinct from one another.

As a distinct person, the Holy Spirit has lived in a love relationship with the Father and Son from all eternity. God created us to participate in that love relationship. God wants us to enjoy fellowship with Him,[17] as each member of the Trinity has enjoyed fellowship with the others from before the beginning of time.[18]

The Spirit Is at Work in the World and in Your Heart Today.

The Holy Spirit speaks to us because He is the third Person of the Trinity, sent by the Father and the Son to work in our hearts. The Holy Spirit has been working for a long, long time. He was active in creation.[19] He inspired the Holy Scriptures.[20] What does He do today? He convicts the world of sin.[21] He regenerates the

---

15 **John 16:13** "However, when He, the Spirit of truth, has come, He will guide you into all truth."
16 **Mark 1:10-11** "And immediately, coming up from the water, He saw the heavens parting and the Spirit descending on Him like a dove. Then a voice came from heaven, 'You are My beloved Son, in whom I am well pleased.'"
17 **1 John 1:4** "Our fellowship *is* with the Father and with His Son Jesus Christ."
18 In John 17:22-23, Jesus speaks of the communion He has with the Father and would like to have with us: "And the glory which You gave Me I have given them, that they may be one just as We are one: I in them, and You in Me; that they may be made perfect in one, and that the world may know that You have sent Me, and have loved them as You have loved Me."
19 **Genesis 1:2** "The earth was without form, and void; and darkness was on the face of the deep. And the Spirit of God was hovering over the face of the waters."
20 According to 2 Peter 1:21, the prophets were moved upon by the Holy Spirit when they wrote the Scriptures. According to 2 Timothy 3:16, the Bible is actually God-breathed. The Bible was inspired in such a way that the words of Scripture are actually the very words of God. See chapter 1 of this book.
21 **John 16:8** "And when He has come, He will convict the world of sin, and of righteousness, and of judgment."

repentant believer[22] and gives assurance to those of us who are saved.[23] He sanctifies us.[24] More specifically, He purifies our hearts as we trust Him for cleansing.[25] He fills us with His presence.[26] He gives us power to live holy lives[27] and to be witnesses for God.[28] He helps us understand the Bible.[29] He enables us to exhibit the "fruit of the Spirit."[30] He gives gifts[31] to each member of the church, so that each of us in the "body" can contribute as the Spirit desires. He "seals" us for the day of redemption,[32] guaranteeing our inheritance in heaven.

Personal Application

Are you allowing God the Holy Spirit to work in your life? Have you let Him purify your heart? Has He given you power to be an effective witness? Are you manifesting the "fruit of the Spirit?" Have you discovered the spiritual gifts that the Spirit has given you? Are you letting Him use you in the body of Christ?

We were made to have the Holy Spirit take up personal residence inside us. We can have a joyful life filled with the presence of the Spirit. We should listen carefully for the Spirit, for He loves to encourage and empower those who are willing to obey His voice.

---

22 **Titus 3:5** "Not by works of righteousness which we have done, but according to His mercy He saved us, through the washing of regeneration and renewing of the Holy Spirit."
23 **Romans 8:16** "The Spirit Himself bears witness with our spirit that we are children of God."
24 **1 Peter 1:2** ". . . sanctification of the Spirit."
25 **Acts 15:9** "And made no distinction between us and them, purifying their hearts by faith."
26 **Acts 2:4** "And they were all filled with the Holy Spirit and began to speak with other tongues, as the Spirit gave them utterance."
27 **Ephesians 3:16** "That He would grant you, according to the riches of His glory, to be strengthened with might through His Spirit in the inner man."
28 **Acts 1:8** "But you shall receive power when the Holy Spirit has come upon you; and you shall be witnesses to Me in Jerusalem, and in all Judea and Samaria, and to the end of the earth."
29 **1 Corinthians 2:14** "But the natural man does not receive the things of the Spirit of God, for they are foolishness to him; nor can he know them, because they are spiritually discerned."
30 **Galatians 5:22** "The fruit of the Spirit is love, joy, peace, longsuffering, kindness, goodness, faithfulness, gentleness, and self-control."
31 There are four groupings of spiritual gifts (gifts of the Spirit). They are in 1 Corinthians 12:8-10, 1 Corinthians 12:29-30, Romans 12:6-8, and Ephesians 4:11.
32 **Ephesians 4:30** "And do not grieve the Holy Spirit of God, by whom you were sealed for the day of redemption."

Some Questions and Answers

➡ Q: *Does Christ live in us or does the Holy Spirit?*

A: Both. Actually, the Father does as well. Jesus said that He and the Father would come to make their abode with those who were willing to obey Him.[33] They accompany the Holy Spirit, whom they send into our lives.

➡ Q: *Then why do we say that the Holy Spirit is the Person who is working in our hearts?*

A: We say that because He is in our hearts to reveal to us the Father and the Son, who are also in us. It is by the Holy Spirit that we come to know Christ. This knowledge is not just knowledge about Christ. We actually come to know Christ *personally* because of the work of the Holy Spirit.

➡ Q: *Do I possess the Holy Spirit when I am saved, or do I have to wait for a second work of grace?*

A: You possess the Holy Spirit when you are saved. Romans 8:9 says that if you don't have the Spirit you don't belong to Jesus.

➡ Q: *How do I receive the Spirit in His fullness?*

A: Jesus said that He would give the Holy Spirit to those who asked.[34] But you must fully surrender to the will of God for your life.[35] Give God everything; then in faith, ask Him to come. He is faithful to keep His promises.[36]

---

[33] **John 14:23** "Jesus answered and said to him, 'If anyone loves Me, he will keep My word; and My Father will love him, and We will come to him and make Our home with him.'"
[34] **Luke 11:13** "If you then, being evil, know how to give good gifts to your children, how much more will your heavenly Father give the Holy Spirit to those who ask Him!"
[35] **Romans 6:12-13** "Therefore do not let sin reign in your mortal body, that you should obey it in its lusts. And do not present your members as instruments of unrighteousness to sin, but present yourselves to God as being alive from the dead, and your members as instruments of righteousness to God."
[36] **1 Thessalonians 5:23-24** "Now may the very God of peace Himself sanctify you completely; and may your whole spirit, soul, and body be preserved blameless at the coming of our Lord Jesus Christ. He who calls you is faithful, who also will do it."

> **I Believe . . .**
> The Holy Spirit is the third Person of the Divine Trinity. Therefore He is God, He is a Person, and He is distinct from the Son and the Father, from whom He proceeds. He convicts the world of sin, and He regenerates the repentant, believing heart. He entirely sanctifies the consecrated believer and brings assurance, guidance, and power to all those born of Him.

Questions for Study

1. What attributes of personality show that the Holy Spirit is a person?
2. What is some scriptural evidence that the Holy Spirit is God?
3. Why is it important to believe that the Spirit is a Divine Person?
4. What are some activities of the Holy Spirit now?
5. What members of the Trinity live in the believer?
6. When does a person receive the Holy Spirit?
7. How can a believer receive the Holy Spirit in His fullness?

Recommended Reading

Murray, Andrew. *Andrew Murray on the Holy Spirit.* New Kesington, PA: Whitaker House, 1998.

Carter, Charles. *The Person and Ministry of the Holy Spirit: A Wesleyan Perspective.* Grand Rapids: Baker Book House, 1974.

8

Satan—Our Chief Enemy

Who Is He?

Is he dressed in black or red? Does he carry a pitchfork and drag a forked tail? We don't know much about Satan's appearance, but we do know that he is a master of disguise. He is like a roaring lion seeking to devour,[1] yet he may seem to be an angel of light when he wants to deceive.[2]

Satan is a spirit. As such, questions about physical appearance may not make much sense; at least, we don't know much about what limitations spirits have on their appearance.

Satan was once an angel in the presence of God. He was created beautiful and holy. But Satan became envious of the glory and sovereignty of God. He decided to go independent and tried to set himself up as an equal to God. He rebelled against God, and many of the other angels followed him.[3] They are now "fallen angels," evil spirits, sometimes called "demons" or "devils," though the term *devil* is most often applied to Satan himself.

What Does He Think of Us?

Satan hates God and therefore hates man, who is created in the image of God and is the object of God's greatest favors. He seeks to bring as many people as possible under the same con-

---

[1] **1 Peter 5:8** "Be sober, be vigilant; because your adversary the devil walks about like a roaring lion, seeking whom he may devour."
[2] **2 Corinthians 11:14** "And no wonder! For Satan himself transforms himself into an angel of light."
[3] **Revelation 12:4** "His tail drew a third of the stars of heaven and threw them to the earth … ."

demnation that he has received by influencing them to rebel against God.

Those who consciously serve Satan are the most deluded people in the world, for they are in a rebellion that cannot succeed, and they are serving a master who hates them and is interested only in destroying them. He makes promises that he knows he cannot fulfill.

Others follow Satan unconsciously when they choose to live in sin. That is why he devotes much time and energy to temptation and deception. He wants to cause people to reject faith in God, making idols of created things instead of worshipping God. His temptations are deceptions, because he really has nothing to offer but perversions of what God has created. The devil has created no joys or pleasures: God created them all. The devil can only offer them in abused forms that are out of the will of God.

What Is He Doing?

Satan is called the "ruler of this world," because the people of this world are mostly in rebellion against God.[4] He claims ownership of the kingdoms of the world, giving them temporarily to whomever he chooses.[5] However, he is already condemned,[6] and all who join him will eventually be condemned with him. The eternal lake of fire was created for Satan and his angels.[7]

He is called the "accuser of our brethren" because he brings charges against believers, trying to get them condemned for sins they have committed.[8]

---

4 **John 12:31** "Now is the judgment of this world; now the ruler of this world will be cast out."
5 **Luke 4:5-6** "Then the devil, taking Him up on a high mountain, showed Him all the kingdoms of the world in a moment of time. And the devil said to Him, 'All this authority I will give You, and their glory; for this has been delivered to me, and I give it to whomever I wish.'"
6 **John 16:11** "... of judgment, because the ruler of this world is judged."
7 **Matthew 25:41** "Then He will also say to those on the left hand, 'Depart from Me, you cursed, into the everlasting fire prepared for the devil and his angels.'"
8 **Revelation 12:10** "... for the accuser of our brethren, who accused them before our God day and night, has been cast down."

Satan desires worship.[9] That is because of his envy of and rivalry with God. He and other demons operate within false religions, receiving worship for themselves.[10] Therefore, we should not think of false religions as merely intellectual errors, but as spiritual blindness. Rarely do those who follow a false religion understand what they are really worshipping. The Bible tells us that the "god of this world" has blinded their eyes.[11]

> **Satan desires worship.**

What about "Possession"?

Satan and other demons try to take full control of people's minds and behavior. This is called "demon possession." Some people have yielded themselves consciously to this kind of possession; perhaps others have allowed it without realizing what they were doing. Some people have gone step by step into this condition, thinking that they were acquiring powers to use for their own purposes. A person so possessed becomes a slave of evil spirits, impelled to self-destruction, and suffering horrible torments of mind and emotions.[12] Only Jesus can deliver a person from this bondage.

In countries where the gospel has been widely preached, the activity of evil spirits is usually disguised. Ironically, it is in these "civilized" countries that people are the most secular, ridiculing anything supernatural and denying the existence of spirits. In such an environment, evil spirits do not act openly, for if they terrified people who have heard the gospel, many of those people would turn to God for deliverance and protection.

---

9 **Matthew 4:9** "And he said to Him, 'All these things will I give You if You will fall down and worship me.'"
10 **1 Corinthians 10:20** "But I say that the things which the Gentiles sacrifice they sacrifice to demons and not to God, and I do not want you to have fellowship with demons."
11 **2 Corinthians 4:4** "Whose minds the god of this age has blinded, who do not believe, lest the light of the gospel of the glory of Christ, who is the image of God, should shine on them."
12 **Mark 5:2-5** "There met him a man with an unclean spirit . . . . And always, night and day, he was in the mountains and in the tombs, crying out and cutting himself with stones."

In countries where the gospel is little known, evil spirits operate openly. The people there do not know that they can turn to Christ for deliverance, so the powers of demons intimidate them and bring them into submission. They serve the spirits, not willingly and joyfully, but fearfully. The gospel comes as a wonderful message of deliverance and freedom.

An Opposite of God?

The devil has power far beyond what humans have in their present, mortal state. However, his power is nothing compared to God's. He should not be thought of as opposite to God, as if he is equal in power. Some philosophers think that the forces for good and evil in the world are approximately equal. That is far from the truth. Satan is not present everywhere, does not know all things, and makes mistakes. God is the Creator of spirits (which were all originally holy and good), and they cannot thwart Him. When the time of man's probation is finished, all evil spirits will be judged, confined, and punished, along with sinful men.

> **Satan's power is nothing compared to God's.**

There are two passages besides the other verses cited in this chapter that seem to speak of Satan and give some details about his fall.

Isaiah 14:12-17

This passage comes in the context of describing the fall and judgment of the king of Babylon. Some of it obviously refers to a human king. However, starting in verse 12, the description seems to parallel the fall of Satan too closely to be coincidental. It seems that the prophet is by inspiration drawing a parallel between the self-exaltation of the king of Babylon and that of the devil. This passage refers to the devil as "Lucifer, son of the morning."

Ezekiel 28:12-19

This passage is similar to the one in Isaiah. It follows a passage addressed to the "prince of Tyre," who was obviously a human king. The next passage is addressed to the "king of Tyre" who may have been the same person, yet, as in the passage in Isaiah, the description seems to go beyond that of a human king to describe the pride and fall of the devil.

In this passage he is said to have been full of wisdom and perfect in beauty, covered with precious stones, a musician with instruments made for him by God the day he was created, the anointed cherub who walked in the fiery stones on the mountain of God. Such a description gives us an idea of the heights from which he fell. We should have a sense of sorrow that such a magnificent creature of God became degraded to what he is now. But this is the result of his sin, and the result is the same for those of mankind who choose sin instead of God.

I Believe . . .
Satan was created to be a holy angel, but rebelled against God. He now is a tempter, deceiver, and accuser, seeking to destroy mankind. As a created being, his power does not compare to God's. He cannot triumph against God, but is already condemned to eternal judgment.

Questions for Study

1. What is the origin of Satan?
2. Why do we not know for sure what Satan looks like?
3. Why does Satan hate man?
4. What does the devil offer in temptation?
5. What is Satan's final destiny?

6. Why do some people yield to demon possession?

7. Why does Satan not reveal himself more openly in "civilized" countries?

Recommended Reading

Lewis, C. S. *The Screwtape Letters.* New York: Macmillan Co., 1968.

Wesley, John. "Satan's Devices." *Wesley's 52 Standard Sermons.* Salem, OH: Schmul Publishing, 1988.

9

Salvation: God's Provision

God the Father planned our salvation even before He created the universe.[1] He knew that we would sin and become His enemies. Yet He chose to love us and to send His only Son to die for us so that we could be saved.[2] Jesus is called "the Lamb slain from the foundation of the world."[3] At the heart of the Good News is God's love for us—not just the Father's love in sending His only Son, but also Jesus' love in laying down His life for us.[4]

Why was such a tremendous price necessary for our salvation? Because of the seriousness of our sin. In order for us to appreciate the Good News about God's provision for our salvation, we have to understand the bad news about our problem.

The Bad News

The bad news is that we are all sinful by nature and by choice. We are slaves to sin.[5] Sinners may think they can quit sinning whenever they want, but it is not true. They are enslaved to sin, and they couldn't stop on their own even if they wanted to. This

---

[1] **Ephesians 1:4** "Just as He chose us in Him before the foundation of the world, that we should be holy and without blame before Him in love."
[2] **John 3:16** "For God so loved the world that He gave His only begotten Son, that whoever believes in Him should not perish but have everlasting life."
[3] **Revelation 13:8** "All who dwell on the earth will worship him, whose names have not been written in the Book of Life of the Lamb slain from the foundation of the world."
[4] **John 15:13** "Greater love has no one than this, than to lay down one's life for his friends."
[5] **Romans 6:19-20** "I speak in human *terms* because of the weakness of your flesh. For just as you presented your members *as* slaves of uncleanness, and of lawlessness *leading* to *more* lawlessness, so now present your members *as* slaves *of* righteousness for holiness. For when you were slaves of sin, you were free in regard to righteousness."

slavery is also described as being under the "power of darkness."[6]

We have broken God's law and are alienated and enemies of God.[7] Few sinners actually think of themselves as God's enemies, but that is how God views them. They are opposed to doing what God wants them to do. As a result they are alienated or separated from God, just like an outlaw is alienated from the law. This is why the Bible says we are "dead in trespasses and sins."[8] To be "alive" spiritually is to know God personally and have a right relationship with Him.[9] Therefore, to be "dead" spiritually means that you don't know God personally and that you don't have a right relationship with Him. Apart from God's grace, we wouldn't even want to be in a right relationship with God.[10]

Our understanding is darkened and our hearts are blinded.[11] We cannot see life and spiritual matters properly (from God's perspective). That is why many sinners talk about not being able to "understand" certain truths that the Bible teaches, like how a loving God can send people to an eternal Hell.

> **The bad news is that we are all sinful by nature and by choice.**

We are all dying physically.[12] We have already been judged for not believing on Jesus,[13] and we have been sentenced to spiritual death and separation from God in Hell and then the Lake of Fire

---

6 **Colossians 1:13** "He has delivered us from the power of darkness and conveyed *us* into the kingdom of the Son of His love."
7 **Romans 5:10** "For if when we were enemies we were reconciled to God through the death of His Son, much more, having been reconciled, we shall be saved by His life."
8 **Ephesians 2:1** "And you *He made alive,* who were dead in trespasses and sins."
9 **John 17:3** "And this is eternal life, that they may know You, the only true God, and Jesus Christ whom You have sent."
10 **Psalm 10:4** "The wicked in his proud countenance does not seek *God;* God *is* in none of his thoughts."
11 **Ephesians 4:18** "Having their understanding darkened, being alienated from the life of God, because of the ignorance that is in them, because of the blindness of their heart."
12 Romans 5:12.
13 **John 3:18** "He who believes in Him is not condemned; but he who does not believe is condemned already, because he has not believed in the name of the only begotten Son of God."

forever.[14] And to make things worse, apart from God's grace, we are unable and unwilling to do anything about our sinfulness.[15]

The Good News: God's Provision

The Good News is that God has provided a way for us to be saved—not just from the penalty of sin, but also from its power over us and ultimately from even its presence. In this chapter we will look at three important aspects of God's provision for our salvation: its nature, its purpose, and its extent.

The Nature of God's Provision

God has provided for our salvation by means of a sacrifice. He set up the sacrificial system in the Old Testament in order to teach His people about the ultimate sacrifice that Jesus, the Lamb of God, would make on the cross. The OT sacrificial system teaches us the following things about the nature of God's provision.

➡ 1. *God is both just and merciful.* God's justice requires that sin be punished. The punishment for sin is death: "The soul that sins shall die."[16] That is why the sacrificial lamb had to die. On the other hand, God's mercy and love moved Him to forgive us and save us from eternal punishment.[17] That is why He promised forgiveness in response to sacrifice. Yet we know that the blood of animals could never take away the sin of humans.[18] For God to simply forgive us without a just basis would make Him unjust and would deny the seriousness of sin. How could God be just and merciful at the same time?

---

14 **Romans 3:23** "For all have sinned and fall short of the glory of God."
15 **Romans 3:10-11** "As it is written: There is none righteous, no, not one; There is none who understands; there is none who seeks after God."
16 **Ezekiel 18:4** "Behold, all souls are Mine; /The soul of the father as well as the soul of the son is Mine; /The soul who sins shall die."
17 **Ephesians 2:4-5** "But God, who is rich in mercy, because of His great love with which He loved us, even when we were dead in trespasses, made us alive together with Christ (by grace you have been saved)."
18 **Hebrews 10:4** "For *it is* not possible that the blood of bulls and goats could take away sins."

Jesus' sacrifice was God's solution to the dilemma of justice and mercy. His death on the cross demonstrates both God's justice—the penalty for sin was paid—mercy—Jesus provided a means for our sins to be forgiven and made it freely available to all.

➤ 2. *Salvation required a perfect sacrifice and the shedding of blood.* Salvation depended on a sacrifice, but not just anything would do. The sacrifice had to meet God's exact specifications. It had to be perfect. In order for Jesus to "take away the sin of the world" He had to be absolutely sinless.[19] The Father provided His Son as the spotless, sinless Lamb of God.[20] Hebrews tells us that without the shedding of blood there is no forgiveness.[21] A bloodless death would not have met God's standard. In order to cleanse us from our sins, Jesus' blood had to be shed.

➤ 3. *Salvation involved a substitutionary sacrifice.* Just as the lamb took the place of the one offering it in the Old Testament, Jesus took our place on the cross.[22] He is our substitute. This is one of the ways we know that the Old Testament sacrifices were only symbols of what Jesus would do. Because a lamb is not an adequate substitute for a man, the Old Testament sacrifices did not really take away sin.[23] There had to be a perfect man who would take our place. This is one of the reasons Jesus became a man—so He could be our perfect substitute.[24] Just as the one making a sacrifice in the Old

---

19 **John 1:29** "The next day John saw Jesus coming toward him, and said, 'Behold! The Lamb of God who takes away the sin of the world!'"
20 **2 Corinthians 5:21** "For He made Him who knew no sin *to be* sin for us, that we might become the righteousness of God in Him."

Hebrews 4:15 "For we do not have a High Priest who cannot sympathize with our weaknesses, but was in all *points* tempted as *we are, yet* without sin."
21 **Hebrews 9:22** "And according to the law almost all things are purified with blood, and without shedding of blood there is no remission." The word *remission* means "forgiveness."
22 **John 11:50** "Nor do you consider that it is expedient for us that one man should die for the people, and not that the whole nation should perish."
23 **Hebrews 10:4** "For *it is* not possible that the blood of bulls and goats could take away sins."
24 **Hebrews 2:17** "Therefore, in all things He had to be made like *His* brethren, that He might be a merciful and faithful High Priest in things *pertaining* to God, to make propitiation for the sins of the people."

Testament received the benefit of the lamb's symbolic death, we receive the benefit of Jesus' death.[25]

➡ 4. *Salvation required a divine sacrifice.* No mortal man, even if he were perfect, could be a sacrifice that would atone for the sins of the whole world. Further, no finite person could provide a sacrifice that would be sufficient for the infinite offense of our sin against our infinitely holy God. Our sacrifice had to be divine.

The Purpose of God's Provision

The word that is normally used for God's provision is *atonement*. The word *atonement* means "at-one-ness." In other words, one of God's purposes in the atonement is to bring fallen mankind back into the unity of a relationship with Himself.[26]

God had many purposes for the salvation He provided. It began the restoration of the created universe from the effects of sin.[27] It inaugurated the Kingdom of God on earth that will some day fill the new heavens and new earth.[28] The primary purpose of the atonement was to deal with the problem of our sin so that we could be reconciled to God and live in holy, loving fellowship with Him for eternity.[29] The Good News is that the salvation God has provided meets every facet of our need. The following statements highlight some of the key aspects of God's purpose for the

---

25 **John 3:14-16** "And as Moses lifted up the serpent in the wilderness, even so must the Son of Man be lifted up, that whoever believes in Him should not perish but have eternal life. For God so loved the world that He gave His only begotten Son, that whoever believes in Him should not perish but have everlasting life."

26 **John 17:20-21** "I do not pray for these alone, but also for those who will believe in Me through their word; that they all may be one, as You, Father, are in Me, and I in You; that they also may be one in Us, that the world may believe that You sent Me."

27 **Romans 8:20-21** "For the creation was subjected to futility, not willingly, but because of Him who subjected *it* in hope; because the creation itself also will be delivered from the bondage of corruption into the glorious liberty of the children of God."

28 **1 Corinthians 15:24-25** "Then *comes* the end, when He delivers the kingdom to God the Father, when He puts an end to all rule and all authority and power. For [Christ] must reign till He has put all enemies under His feet." See also Daniel 2:24-45; 7:14, 26-27.

29 **2 Corinthians 5:18-19** "Now all things *are* of God, who has reconciled us to Himself through Jesus Christ, and has given us the ministry of reconciliation, that is, that God was in Christ reconciling the world to Himself, not imputing their trespasses to them, and has committed to us the word of reconciliation."

atonement in relation to us. Special terms for these facets of salvation are underlined.

- ◆ Our relationship with God was broken, and we were at war with God; Jesus made it possible for our relationship to be restored. He <u>reconciled</u> us to God, making peace.[30]

- ◆ We were condemned sinners, deserving to die; Jesus died in our place, setting us <u>free</u> from the punishment we deserved and from the power of sin.[31]

- ◆ We had a record of sins; Jesus' blood <u>expiated</u> the record—that is, He wiped it clean. Now there is no record of sins held against us.[32]

- ◆ God was justly and righteously angry with us because of our sin; Jesus' death <u>propitiated</u> God's wrath against us, satisfying Him and turning His wrath away.[33]

- ◆ We were slaves to sin; Jesus <u>redeemed</u> us—paid the price to free us from sin's power.[34]

- ◆ We are all dying physically; Jesus' resurrection guarantees that we too will be <u>resurrected</u> and glorified with new bodies just like His. This is a part of salvation that the believer does not receive immediately, but waits for in faith.[35]

---

[30] **Romans 5:1, 10** "Therefore, having been justified by faith, we have peace with God through our Lord Jesus Christ, ... For if when we were enemies we were reconciled to God through the death of His Son, much more, having been reconciled, we shall be saved by His life."

[31] **Romans 5:6-8** "For when we were still without strength, in due time Christ died for the ungodly. For scarcely for a righteous man will one die; yet perhaps for a good man someone would even dare to die. But God demonstrates His own love toward us, in that while we were still sinners, Christ died for us."

[32] **Hebrews 8:12** "For I will be merciful to their unrighteousness, and their sins and their lawless deeds I will remember no more."

[33] **1 John 2:2** "And He Himself is the propitiation for our sins, and not for ours only but also for the whole world."

[34] **Luke 1:74** "To grant us that we, being delivered from the hand of our enemies, might serve Him without fear, in holiness and righteousness before Him all the days of our life." See also Romans 6:6, 11, 12, 14.

[35] **2 Corinthians 4:14** "Knowing that He who raised up the Lord Jesus will also raise us up with Jesus, and will present *us* with you."

The Extent of God's Provision

When God sent Jesus to die for the world, He intended to provide salvation for all men. God is not willing that anyone should perish.[36] It was because of God's love for the world that He provided a perfect sacrifice for our sins and, "not for ours only but also for [the sins of] the whole world."[37]

This is the reason Jesus is called "the Savior of all men, especially of those who believe."[38] He is the Savior of "all men" because He has provided salvation for every person who has ever been born. Titus 2:11 says the grace of God that brings salvation has appeared to *all men*. But He is the Savior of "those who believe" in a special sense because He has actually saved them from their sins.

Of course, though God has made this provision for all men and freely invites all into a relationship with Him, many do not accept it. Men are both unwilling and unable to come to God, apart from His grace, but God gives all men enough grace that they are able to respond to the Good News of salvation.[39]

In our next chapter we will look at our response to God's provision and what God does for us when we respond.

I Believe . . .
God provided Jesus as a perfect sacrifice to take our place and shed His blood so that we might be forgiven, reconciled to God, freed from sin's power, and brought into holy, loving fellowship with God. Jesus' sacrifice provided an eternal salvation that is sufficient for all men but applies only to those who repent and believe.

---

36 **2 Peter 3:9** "The Lord is not slack concerning *His* promise, as some count slackness, but is longsuffering toward us, not willing that any should perish but that all should come to repentance."
37 **1 John 2:2** "And He Himself is the propitiation for our sins, and not for ours only but also for the whole world."
38 **1 Timothy 4:10** "For to this *end* we both labor and suffer reproach, because we trust in the living God, who is *the* Savior of all men, especially of those who believe."
39 **Titus 2:11** "For the grace of God that brings salvation has appeared to all men."

Questions for Study

1. When did God plan our salvation?
2. List five aspects of the bad news about man's condition apart from God.
3. What does the Old Testament sacrificial system teach us about God's provision for our salvation?
4. How does Jesus' death on the cross demonstrate God's justice and His mercy?
5. Why did Jesus actually have to shed His blood when He died?
6. What does the word **atonement** mean?
7. What is the primary purpose of the atonement?
8. What does it mean that we are reconciled to God?
9. What does it mean that God is propitiated?
10. What does it mean that we are redeemed?
11. What passage teaches us that Jesus died for the sins of the whole world and not just for our sins?
12. What verse teaches that grace for salvation has been revealed to everyone?

Recommended Reading

Purkiser, W. T., ed. *Exploring Our Christian Faith*. Kansas City, MO: Beacon Hill Press, 1960. Especially see chapter XI, "Man's Predicament," and XII, "The Doctrine of Atonement."

Wilcox, Leslie. *Profiles in Wesleyan Theology*. Salem, OH: Schmul Publishing, 1985. Especially see chapters 9-10: "Atonement" and "Conditions of Reconciliation," 171-214.

Wiley, H. Orton, and Culbertson, Paul T. *Introduction to Christian Theology*. Kansas City, MO: Beacon Hill Press, 1946. Especially see chapter XIII, "Atonement."

10

Salvation: God's Work and Our Response

God has provided an atonement so that anyone in the world can be saved. Unfortunately, not everyone is saved. The reason is that some people refuse to meet the conditions God says must be met before He will save a person.

Perhaps the most important thing you should know about our salvation is that it depends entirely upon God's grace. God's gracious work comes before, during, and after our response to the Gospel. In this chapter, we will look at three aspects of God's work and our response: (1) what God does to prepare us to be saved, (2) what response He requires from us, and (3) what He does when we meet His conditions for salvation.

God's Work of Preparation

God's work toward saving us begins with what theologians call "prevenient grace." The word *prevenient* means "to go before, to go ahead of." Grace is anything God gives us that we do not deserve. The prevenient grace God gives us before we are saved is primarily the desire and power to respond to His truth.

Everyone in the world receives prevenient grace. Titus 2:11 says that "the grace of God that brings salvation has appeared to all men."[1] We receive this grace first through God's revelation of

---

[1] This appears to be what John is talking about when he says, "That [Jesus] was the true Light which gives light to every man coming into the world" (John 1:9).

Himself in nature and in our consciences.[2] Romans 1:20 makes it clear that anyone who does not respond to the light of nature and conscience will have no excuse when he stands before God.

> **Grace is anything God gives us that we do not deserve.**

As part of giving prevenient grace to all men, God draws sinners to Himself.[3] In fact, no one can come to Christ unless the Father draws him.[4] The Holy Spirit opens our hearts to pay attention to and understand the gospel call.[5] He convicts our consciences of guilt, makes us aware of God's justice, and shows us the penalty for sin.[6] He shows us that there is hope for salvation through what Christ has done for us in the atonement.[7] God also enables us to repent and to believe the Gospel.[8]

The Response God Requires from Us

Even though God enables us to repent and have faith, He doesn't repent or believe for us, or force us to do so. We must act

---

2 **Romans 1:20-21** "For since the creation of the world His invisible *attributes* are clearly seen, being understood by the things that are made, *even* His eternal power and Godhead, so that they are without excuse, because, although they knew God, they did not glorify *Him* as God, nor were thankful, but became futile in their thoughts, and their foolish hearts were darkened."
3 **John 12:32** "If I [Jesus] am lifted up from the earth, I will draw all men to Myself."
4 **John 6:44** "No one can come to Me unless the Father who sent Me draws him; and I will raise him up at the last day."
5 **1 Corinthians 2:14** "But the natural man does not receive the things of the Spirit of God, for they are foolishness to him; nor can he know *them,* because they are spiritually discerned."
6 **John 16:8-11** "And when [the Comforter] has come, He will convict the world of sin, and of righteousness, and of judgment: of sin, because they do not believe in Me; of righteousness, because I go to My Father and you see Me no more; of judgment, because the ruler of this world is judged."
7 **Colossians 1:5** "Because of the hope which is laid up for you in heaven, of which you heard before in the word of the truth of the gospel."
8 **Acts 11:18** "When they heard these things they became silent; and they glorified God, saying, 'Then God has also granted to the Gentiles repentance to life.'"

upon God's gracious enabling. God will not save anyone who is not willing to repent and believe.[9]

Since repentance and faith are the two conditions[10] God has set for saving us, we need to understand what they are.[11] Repentance is not just feeling bad about our sins. It means that we admit we are guilty and deserve punishment. It is a change of mind that results in a change of behavior. When you repent, you change your mind about following after sin. This change of mind must be evidenced by subsequent turning from sin, following Jesus, and doing what is right.[12] If it is not, it is not repentance.

The faith that is necessary for salvation is believing in Jesus. When we believe in Jesus, we are not just saying, "Yes, I believe that Jesus was the Son of God," like we believe that George Washington was the first president of the United States. Faith has three elements to it. (1) It believes that what God has said is true. (2) It commits to do what He requires. (3) It trusts in and rests on what God has promised.[13] It is important to remember that our faith does not earn or merit us salvation. Faith is a condition God has set for saving us. Meeting God's condition does not earn us anything. It doesn't even make us "better" than someone who fails to meet God's condition of faith.[14]

---

9 **John 5:39-40** "You search the Scriptures, for in them you think you have eternal life; and these are they which testify of Me. But you are not willing to come to Me that you may have life."
10 Technically repentance is a prerequisite for faith, and faith alone is the condition of salvation. However, since there can be no faith apart from repentance, one may speak of faith and repentance as conditions for salvation.
11 **Isaiah 55:7** "Let the wicked forsake his way, /And the unrighteous man his thoughts; /Let him return to the LORD, /And He will have mercy on him; /And to our God, /For He will abundantly pardon."
   Acts 3:19 "Repent therefore and be converted, that your sins may be blotted out, so that times of refreshing may come from the presence of the Lord."
12 **1 Thessalonians 1:9** "For they themselves declare concerning us what manner of entry we had to you, and how you turned to God from idols to serve the living and true God." The context of 1 Thess. 1 makes it clear that this is Paul's description of the Thessalonians' repentance.
13 **Hebrews 11:6** "But without faith *it is* impossible to please *Him*, for he who comes to God must believe that He is, and *that* He is a rewarder of those who diligently seek Him."
14 **Romans 4:4-5** "Now to him who works, the wages are not counted as grace but as debt. But to him who does not work but believes on Him who justifies the ungodly, his faith is accounted for righteousness."

You might wonder, "How are the elements of faith expressed in the faith that is necessary for salvation?" (1) To believe what God said, you have to believe that Jesus is the Son of God, that His sacrifice on the cross was sufficient for your sins, and that He rose bodily from the grave.[15] (2) To commit to obeying God, you have to be willing to leave your sins and begin serving God. (3) To trust His promises, you must believe that He does forgive you when you have met His requirements for salvation. God has promised that whoever believes on the Lord Jesus Christ will be saved.[16]

> Meeting God's condition does not earn us anything.

God's Work after We Respond

When we repent and believe, God saves us. The experience of being saved from sin, being reconciled to God, and entering a new relationship with Him can take place very simply. And yet God does many things all at the same time when He saves us. Even though God does all of the following things at the same time, we can put them in logical order: God unites us with Christ, justifies us, sanctifies (regenerates) us, adopts us, and seals us with the Holy Spirit.

Salvation involves quite a lot! The reason for this is that there were so many things wrong with us. We may not ever fully understand our salvation in this life, and we don't have to understand it completely in order to benefit from it. But the more we understand, the more we can appreciate what God has done for us. Let's look at each of the elements of God's work in their logical order.

---

[15] **1 John 4:15** "Whoever confesses that Jesus is the Son of God, God abides in him, and he in God."

[16] **Romans 10:9** "That if you confess with your mouth [that Jesus is Lord] and believe in your heart that God has raised Him from the dead, you will be saved."

→ First, God unites us with Jesus. When we believe on Jesus, we are united to Him spiritually like a branch is united to a vine physically.[17] It is through this union that we have spiritual life, for His life is flowing into us.[18] Every single spiritual blessing we enjoy comes to us because we are in Christ.[19] "In Him [Christ] we have redemption through His blood, the forgiveness of our trespasses."[20] "Therefore, if anyone is in Christ, he is a new creature; the old things have passed away; behold, new things have come."[21] This union goes both ways: we are in Christ and Christ is in us.[22] "Christ in us" is the basis for our hope of glory (heaven).[23]

→ Second, He justifies us. *Justify* is not a word we use every day, so it may sound strange at first. But it is a very important word. Because of our sins, we stood condemned in God's courtroom, but Jesus took our chastisement so that we could be counted righteous.[24]

> **We stood condemned in God's courtroom.**

When God justifies us He (1) forgives our sins.[25] In other words, He no longer holds them against us because Jesus

---

17 **John 15:5-6** "I am the vine, you *are* the branches. He who abides in Me, and I in him, bears much fruit; for without Me you can do nothing. If anyone does not abide in Me, he is cast out as a branch and is withered; and they gather them and throw *them* into the fire, and they are burned."
18 **Colossians 3:4** "When Christ *who is* our life appears, then you also will appear with Him in glory."
19 **Ephesians 1:3** "Blessed *be* the God and Father of our Lord Jesus Christ, who has blessed us with every spiritual blessing in the heavenly *places* in Christ."
20 Ephesians 1:7.
21 2 Corinthians 5:17.
22 **John 15:4** "Abide in Me, and I in you. As the branch cannot bear fruit of itself, unless it abides in the vine, neither can you, unless you abide in Me."
23 **Colossians 1:27** "To them God willed to make known what are the riches of the glory of this mystery among the Gentiles: which is Christ in you, the hope of glory."
24 **Isaiah 53:5** "But He *was* wounded for our transgressions, /*He was* bruised for our iniquities; /The chastisement for our peace *was* upon Him, /And by His stripes we are healed."
25 **Romans 4:7** "Blessed *are those* whose lawless deeds are forgiven, And whose sins are covered."

paid for them. (2) He blots out the record of our sins.[26] As far as the record of Heaven shows, there is no sin on our record. (3) He credits our faith as righteousness.[27] (4) He declares us to be righteous,[28] and (5) He accepts us for Christ's sake.[29]

Our justification is based on our union with Christ through faith. Perhaps an illustration will make this clear. Imagine that Susan is hopelessly in debt and as poor as a church mouse. Tom, on the other hand, is a billionaire. Tom and Susan get married. When Susan marries Tom, all of their financial assets and liabilities are combined. Since Tom has more than enough to pay Susan's debts, Susan becomes a billionaire the minute they are married. We were just like Susan. We were hopelessly in debt because of our sins. But when we were united to Christ, immediately all of our debt was paid for by His blood,[30] and we became righteous because He is righteous.[31]

This is what God does *for* us. This is all a legal transaction that has to do with the record of our sin and our guiltiness before God's law.

→ Third, He initially sanctifies us. This is the work of God *in* us. Not only does He declare us righteous (justifying us), but He *makes* us righteous and holy (sanctifies us). This is why Christians are called "saints."[32] Perhaps you are used to thinking of

---

26 **Colossians 2:14** "Having wiped out the handwriting of requirements that was against us, which was contrary to us. And He has taken it out of the way, having nailed it to the cross."
27 **Romans 4:5** "But to him who does not work but believes on Him who justifies the ungodly, his faith is accounted for righteousness."
28 **Romans 3:26** "To demonstrate at the present time His righteousness, that He might be just and the justifier of the one who has faith in Jesus."
29 **Romans 14:3** "The one who eats is not to regard with contempt the one who does not eat, and the one who does not eat is not to judge the one who eats, for God has accepted him." See also Eph. 4:32.
30 **1 Peter 1:18-19** "Knowing that you were not redeemed with corruptible things, *like* silver or gold, from your aimless conduct *received* by tradition from your fathers, but with the precious blood of Christ, as of a lamb without blemish and without spot."
31 **Philippians 3:9** "And be found in Him, not having my own righteousness, which *is* from the law, but that which *is* through faith in Christ, the righteousness which is from God by faith."
32 See Eph. 1:1; Phil. 1:1; Col. 1:1. The term *saint* occurs around 60 times in the NT and emphasizes the fact that a Christian is no longer a sinner, but has been separated unto God and is now holy.

the term *sanctification* as always referring to a second, definite work of grace that God does for us after we are saved. While God can indeed entirely sanctify us (see chapters 11-13), He *initially* sanctifies us when we are saved.[33] Paul said that the Corinthians, though they were still carnal or spiritual babes,[34] had already been sanctified.[35]

Justification refers to a change that is made "on the books" so to speak, changing our legal standing before God. Initial sanctification refers to a real change that happens within us. God sets us apart from our old life of sin, claims us as His own, makes us holy, and begins transforming us into the likeness of Christ. The relationship between justification and initial sanctification can be illustrated by a dollar bill. Justification is like the front side of the bill. Initial sanctification is like the back side of the bill. If you compare the front and back sides of a dollar bill, you will see that each has its specific characteristics and is quite different from the other. We can talk about the differences between the front and back sides, but you do not have a genuine dollar bill unless both sides are present. In the same way, when we are saved, we are justified and initially sanctified at the same time.

When we are initially sanctified, we are actually cleansed on the inside;[36] we are made new creatures;[37] we are born again.[38] Titus 3:5 says that God saves us by "the washing of regeneration." The word *regeneration* means rebirth. The new birth that God gives us is like a washing that removes all the dirt

---

[33] Thomas Ralston, *Elements of Divinity*, 371.
[34] **1 Corinthians 3:1** "And I, brethren, could not speak to you as to spiritual *people* but as to carnal, as to babes in Christ."
[35] **1 Corinthians 1:2** "To the church of God which is at Corinth, to those who are sanctified in Christ Jesus, called *to be* saints, with all who in every place call on the name of Jesus Christ our Lord, both theirs and ours."
[36] **Hebrews 10:22** "Let us draw near with a true heart in full assurance of faith, having our hearts sprinkled from an evil conscience and our bodies washed with pure water."
[37] **2 Corinthians 5:17** "Therefore, if anyone *is* in Christ, *he is* a new creation; old things have passed away; behold, all things have become new."
[38] **John 3:3** "Jesus answered and said to him, 'Most assuredly, I say to you, unless one is born again, he cannot see the kingdom of God.'"

and gives us new life. When we are given new life in Christ, our names are written in Heaven in the Lamb's book of life.[39]

- Fourth, God adopts us. When we are born again, we become part of God's family. We are not made distant relatives, but God's sons and daughters.[40] The Bible speaks of a Christian's being born into God's family as well as being adopted. Although being born into a family and being adopted seem like two different things, these are actually two pictures designed to teach us about our new relationship with God. Earthly adoption includes receiving the full rights of a son. In the same way, in our spiritual adoption, God grants us all the rights and privileges that come with being His children.[41] God could have made us members of His family without giving us all the rights and privileges of being His children. Praise the Lord that He has adopted us!

- Fifth, God seals us with the Holy Spirit.[42] He places His Holy Spirit within us as a seal that identifies us as His children. The Holy Spirit is the agent of God's grace working in us every day. He is the One who makes possible our ongoing relationship with God. He is the down payment and guarantee of the rest of the inheritance God has promised us—eternal life in heaven with God.[43] That's what Ephesians 1:14 means when it says that the Holy Spirit is the "guarantee of our inheritance." God has given us the Holy Spirit to guide us and guard us from sin.[44]

---

[39] **Luke 10:20** "Nevertheless do not rejoice in this, that the spirits are subject to you, but rather rejoice because your names are written in heaven."

[40] **John 1:12** "But as many as received Him, to them He gave the right to become children of God, to those who believe in His name:"

[41] The Bible also uses the term *adoption* to refer to the time in the future when we will receive resurrected bodies (Rom. 8:23).

[42] **Ephesians 1:13** "In Him you also *trusted*, after you heard the word of truth, the gospel of your salvation; in whom also, having believed, you were sealed with the Holy Spirit of promise."

[43] **Ephesians 1:14** "[The Holy Spirit] is the guarantee of our inheritance until the redemption of the purchased possession, to the praise of His glory."

[44] **Galatians 5:16** "I say then: Walk in the Spirit, and you shall not fulfill the lust of the flesh."

Isn't God's work in our salvation wonderful? It is hard to imagine that God would love us even when we were His enemies, but He did. We should be very thankful for our union with Christ, justification, sanctification, adoption, and sealing with the Holy Spirit.

> I Believe . . .
> All men receive God's prevenient grace which gives them the desire to know Him and the power to repent and believe on Jesus. When a sinner is forgiven, he is united with Christ, forgiven of his sins (justified), made righteous (sanctified), brought into God's family (born again and adopted), and sealed with the Holy Spirit.

Questions for Study

1. What does God's work toward saving us begin with?
2. What is grace? What is prevenient grace?
3. What passage of Scripture teaches us that all men have received prevenient grace?
4. Why does a sinner need the Father to draw him to Christ?
5. What are three of the things the Holy Spirit does in preparing us to be saved?
6. What are the two conditions God requires us to meet before He will save us?
7. What is repentance?
8. What is faith?
9. Does meeting the conditions of salvation earn us salvation?
10. How are the three elements of faith expressed in saving faith?
11. What is the logical order of what God does to save us after we repent and believe?

12. What are the five things God does for us when He justifies us?
13. What is our justification based on?
14. What are four of the things God does in us when He initially sanctifies us?
15. What is regeneration?
16. What is the difference between being born again and being adopted by God?
17. What does it mean that God "seals" us with the Holy Spirit?

Recommended Reading

Purkiser, W. T., ed. *Exploring Our Christian Faith.* Kansas City, MO: Beacon Hill Press, 1960. See especially chapter XIV, "The New Life," 287-304.

Ralston, Thomas N. *Elements of Divinity.* Nashville: Abingdon-Cokesbury Press, 1924. See especially chapters 26-28, and 32-35.

Wilcox, Leslie. *Profiles in Wesleyan Theology.* Salem, OH: Schmul Publishing, 1985. See especially chapter 11, "A New Creature in Christ," 215-236.

Wiley, H. Orton and Culbertson, Paul T. *Introduction to Christian Theology.* Kansas City, MO: Beacon Hill Press, 1946. See especially chapter XVI, "Justification, Regeneration, and Adoption," 275-296.

11

An Introduction to Christian Holiness

A Deep Desire

Because God is holy, every true Christian desires to be holy. He has a desire to be thoroughly good, even as God is. This deep desire results in a commitment to live a holy life.

God has imparted this desire to those who are in relationship with Him. A person cannot love and worship God without desiring to have a nature like His.

God expects those who receive the grace of forgiveness through faith in the death and resurrection of Jesus to live lives that conform to His own character—a character that He reveals as holy.

The grace of forgiveness and the grace which transforms the Christian's life come together, never separately.

Why We Should Be Holy

There are four reasons we should be holy, and all of them are based on the will of God for us.

- *God created us to be holy*—Eph. 1:4: "Just as He chose us in Him before the foundation of the world, that we should be holy and without blame before Him in love."
- *God calls us to be holy*—2 Tim. 1:9: "Who has saved us and called with a holy calling."

- *God commands us to be holy*—1 Peter 1:15, 16: "But as He who called you is holy, you also be holy in all your conduct, because it is written, "Be holy, for I am holy."
- *God requires holiness for entry into heaven*—Hebrew 12:14: "Pursue peace with all men, and holiness, without which no one will see the Lord."

How Can Imperfect Humans Be Holy?

Let's acknowledge something at the beginning. We are all imperfect humans. That means that there is plenty of room for improvement. It also means that we are limited and frail. Because of those characteristics of humanity, many people have assumed that holiness is impossible for us.

> When God issues a command He also supplies the grace and power to obey!

God knows our nature, because He created us. Yet it is to imperfect, limited, frail humans that God commands: "Be holy." When God issues a command He also supplies the grace and power to obey!

There are three important grammatical truths about the *command* in 1 Peter 1:15, "Be holy." First, it is a *present tense* command—signifying an on-going, continuous reality for our lives every moment of every day. Secondly, it is *plural in number*—God expects all born-again Christians to be holy. Thirdly, it is in the *imperative mood*—it is a command, not a suggestion.

Three Essential Elements to Holiness

- **(1) To be holy I must be connected to the SOURCE of holiness—God Himself.**

All holiness finds its origin and source in God. God alone is holy (Rev. 15:4, "You alone are holy"; see also Exod. 15:11; Psa. 99:5). Nothing is holy until it is connected to the origin and source of holiness — God Himself. All holiness proceeds from God. The holiness of persons, things, days, and places is caused and sustained only by being in a special relationship with the holy God.

All born-again Christians are connected to the SOURCE of holiness—God—through the new birth. Colossians 3:3 says, "For you died, and your life is hidden with Christ in God." If you are born again, you are "in Christ" (Rom. 8:1). We actually become holy at the new birth because of this connection!

God now calls us "saints." The normal word to describe Christians in the New Testament is *saints*, literally meaning "holy ones."

Do not confuse "holy" or "holiness" with "entire sanctification." Holiness/sanctification begins at the new birth. Entire sanctification is a sub-category of sanctification and refers to the work of God in us after we are saved whereby the Holy Spirit cleanses our heart from inbred sin and takes full control of our lives (1 Thes. 5:23-23; Romans 12:1; Acts 15:9; Eph. 5:18).

➡ **(2) To be holy I must be SEPARATED to God as His possession—I become the property of God.**

"You shall be a special treasure to Me above all people . . . a holy nation." What is holy is claimed by God as His treasure, His possession.[1]

"And you shall be holy to Me: for I the LORD *am* holy, and have separated you from the peoples, that you should be mine."[2]

"You are not your own—for you were bought at a price; therefore glorify God in your body and in your spirit, which are God's."[3]

When a person gets saved, he or she becomes the property of God. God has a right to do what He wants with His property! He has the right to tell us how to live.

This separation that makes me a special person also separates me from the common and ordinary—all that is not dedicated to God.

---

[1] Exodus 19:5, 6.
[2] Leviticus 20:26.
[3] 1 Corinthians 6:19, 20.

Think about what Moses learned when he met God at the burning bush (Exodus 3:5). A common, ordinary bush, rooted in common, ordinary ground, was changed into a holy bush and the ground became holy because the bush and the ground became connected to the source of holiness—God Himself appearing to Moses.

God claimed that ground as His own—He separated it unto Himself. He distinguished that ground from the common, ordinary ground around it, and made it "holy" ground. It was no longer common, ordinary ground. The same is true about us if we are saved!

Here are some verses that show that what is holy is distinguished from the ordinary.

"And the priest answered David, and said, 'There is no common [ordinary] bread on hand; but there is holy bread.'"[4] This was bread that had been dedicated for use in worship of God.

"And they [the priests] shall teach my people the difference between the holy and the [common], and cause them to discern between the unclean and the clean."[5]

God has the right to separate His holy people from common or ordinary things that He knows will not be good for them spiritually.

Another aspect of separation is that we are to be separated from anything that is sinful and that which defiles me in God's eyes.

"For God did not call us to uncleanness, but in holiness."[6]

"For this is the will of God, your sanctification: that you should abstain from sexual immorality."[7]

God expects moral purity in your life. Holiness requires us to stop doing everything and anything that God says is sinful. That

---

[4] 1 Samuel 21:4.
[5] Ezekiel 44:23.
[6] 1 Thessalonians 4:7.
[7] 1 Thessalonians 4:3.

brings us to the third aspect of holiness—sharing in the nature of God.

➡ **(3) To be holy means that I SHARE in the nature of God—I become Christlike.**

What does it mean to be holy like God is? He has most fully shown us what holiness in human form looks like through the character of Christ.[8]

The fundamental character of Christ that God wants us to begin with is a passion to do the will of God. A passion is more than a willingness. Look at these statements that Jesus made.

"My food is to do the will of Him who sent Me, and to finish His work."[9]

"I have glorified You on the earth. I have finished the work which You have given me to do."[10]

"Behold, I have come to do Your will, O God."[11]

So at the foundation of Christlikeness is a passion to fulfill the will of God.

We already know that God expects obedience from those who are holy. In Leviticus 20:7-8, which Peter quoted, God said, "Sanctify yourselves therefore, and be holy, for I am the Lord your God, and you shall keep My statutes, and perform them: I am the Lord who sanctifies you." So in the very same breath that God commands us to be holy, He commands us to obey His word.

You can't be knowingly violating God's word, and say, "I am holy." It's a contradiction of terms. God expects us to walk in the light as He shines it on our path. To be holy requires full obedience to God's word.

---

[8] For a scriptural description of how we should display Christlikeness, see 1 Peter 2:20-24, Ephesians 5:1-2, and Philippians 2:5-8.
[9] John 4:34.
[10] John 17:4.
[11] Hebrews 10:9.

1 Peter 1:14 says that as Christians you are to be "obedient children, not conforming yourselves to the former lusts, as in your ignorance."

What does the phrase "former lusts" refer to? It refers to the values and lifestyles we had before we were saved that were not in conformity to God's word. Before we were saved, our lives were ruled by these desires. This is the worldliness of Romans 12:2 to which we are not to be conformed.

Worldliness is opposed to Christlikeness, for it is any attitude or action that does not conform to God's word.

Holiness prescribes a way of behaving that is determined by the character of God. The character of God is revealed to us in the nature of Christ. To follow Christlikeness is to have a passion to live a life pleasing to God, which will be in contrast to the way of the world.

Three Irreducible Elements of Holiness

◆ **You must be connected to the SOURCE of holiness, God, through the new birth.**

◆ **You must be SEPARATED to God as His possession, separated from what is ordinary and whatever is sinful or defiles.**

◆ **You must SHARE in the nature of God—Christlikeness.**

I Believe . . .
God created us to be holy and calls us back from sin to be made holy by His grace. To be holy is to be in right relationship to God, reserved as His special possession apart from all that is ordinary, separated from all that is sinful and displeasing to God, and sharing in the holy nature of God by being made Christlike.

Questions for Study

1. What is the foundation for our reasons to be holy?
2. Why is our humanness not an excuse for failing to be holy?
3. When can a person be called holy?
4. What are some kinds of separation that are part of holiness?
5. What are the three irreducible elements of holiness?

Recommended Reading

Cattell, Everett. *The Spirit of Holiness.* Grand Rapids: William B. Eerdmans Publishing Co., 1963.

Taylor, Richard S. *Exploring Christian Holiness.* Vol. 3. Kansas City: Beacon Hill Press, 1985.

12

Understanding Entire Sanctification

The young man sat in my office with tears in his eyes. "I'm so confused," he said. "What are you confused about?" He replied, "I know that Jesus has saved me, and I know I love the Lord, but I don't understand what people are talking about when they say you have to be entirely sanctified. What is entire sanctification, and why is it so important?"

The young man's confusion and concern was not surprising to me. For any Christian who is serious about living a holy life, certain questions arise. My hope and prayer is that this chapter will help you understand entire sanctification and experience the peace that comes from a full surrender to God.

Where Did the Phrase Entire Sanctification Come From?

The phrase *entire sanctification* comes from Paul's prayer for the Thessalonian believers in 1 Thessalonians 5:23. The verse reads: "Now may the God of peace Himself <u>sanctify you completely</u>; and may your whole spirit, soul, and body be preserved blameless at the coming of our Lord Jesus Christ." The adverb *completely* means "entirely," or "through and through." Paul's description of a complete sanctification led to the phrase *entire sanctification*.

What Is Entire Sanctification?

Before we can understand entire sanctification, it is necessary to become more familiar with sanctification itself. The most commonly used words in the New Testament to describe the change that occurs at the moment of conversion are derived from the Greek verb *hagiadzo*.[1] The verb is usually translated "sanctify" or "sanctified" and describes God's work in our lives to conform us to the image of Christ. The related noun is frequently translated "sanctification." As it relates to our salvation, *sanctification* can indicate at least three aspects of God's work in our lives: *initial* sanctification, *progressive* sanctification, and *entire* sanctification.[2]

Initial sanctification refers to the work of God through the Holy Spirit at the moment we are born again, by which He sets us apart to Himself as His possession, separates us from the practice of willful sin, and begins the process of making us like Jesus Christ.[3]

Progressive sanctification refers to the on-going work of the Holy Spirit, daily transforming us into the likeness of Christ. Progressive sanctification begins at the moment of conversion and continues throughout life until glorification in heaven.[4]

Entire sanctification refers to a specific further work of God's grace in the life of a Christian by which God cleanses the heart from inherited depravity and fills the Christian with the Holy Spirit, thereby enabling one to love God completely—with all the heart, mind, soul, and strength—and one's neighbor as oneself. This cleansing empowers the Christian to serve Christ more effectively.[5]

---

[1] The verb *hagiadzo* occurs twenty-eight times in the New Testament. It is translated *hallowed* (2 times), *sanctifies* (4 times), *sanctify* (6 times), *sanctified* (15 times), and *let him be holy* (1 time). The related noun *hagiasmos* is translated *sanctification* (5 times) and *holiness* (5 times) and speaks of the relationship a believer has with God that makes him holy.

[2] H. Orton Wiley, *Christian Theology*, (Kansas City: Beacon Hill Press, 1952), II, 464-496.

[3] 1 Corinthians 1:2 and 6:11 call the Corinthians "sanctified" in this sense (see also Acts 20:32; 26:18; Hebrews 10:10).

[4] **Hebrews 2:11** "For both He who sanctifies and those who are being sanctified are all of one, for which reason He is not ashamed to call them brethren" (see also 2 Timothy 2:21; Hebrews 10:14).

[5] Acts 1:8.

How Do We Know that We Need to be Entirely Sanctified?

➡ **Because of the self-centeredness that remains after conversion**

According to Psalm 51:5, we are all born with the desire to have our own way. At the moment of physical conception, as a result of Adam's sin,[6] we inherit a corrupt nature that makes us self-centered and inclined to sin.[7] Self-centeredness is what inevitably leads every one of us, even while we are still children, to reject God's will and seek our own way. It explains the universality of sin in the human race. It is the reason people put their own benefits above the benefits of others, assert their wills against what they know is right, and tend to follow the ways of the sinful world.

At the moment of new birth, we are forgiven for all the sins of our past,[8] and we are united with Christ. However, even after we are saved, self-centeredness continues in our life and causes us spiritual problems, though it does not control us as it did before.[9] Because of this condition of the heart, though we have repented of the actions that we recognize as sin, we still have inner sins such as pride and selfishness.

---

6 Romans 5:12.
7 Various phrases have been used to describe the idea of being born "in sin": inherited depravity, the inner principle of sin, pride, the carnal nature, or double mindedness. Because self-centeredness appears to be the primary manifestation of our corrupt nature, I use the phrase self-centeredness as short hand for inherited depravity through out this chapter.
8 Our past sin is known as *acquired depravity* (cf. 1 John 1:9).
9 In Psalm 51:7, when the Psalmist David prayed, "Purge me with hyssop, and I shall be clean; /Wash me, and I shall be whiter than snow," it was no accident that he chose to use the term *hyssop*. Hyssop was a plant that was used in the ceremonies for cleansing of leprosy (Lev. 14:3-8), cleansing from contact with a dead body (Num. 19:11-22), and in the application of the blood of the Passover lamb to the door posts and lintels in order to protect the inhabitants from the death angel (Ex. 12:22). Evidently David saw the seriousness of the inner depravity with which he had been born (Psalm 51:5) and recognized that it was the root cause of his willful sin against God and his fellow man. He saw that his inner depravity was like the disease of leprosy and was defiling like contact with a dead body. He recognized that God alone could purge his heart from his inherited malady and make him whiter than snow.

The remaining self-centeredness usually reveals itself when God begins probing one's life and revealing attitudes and actions that He wants to change.

Many times the change He wishes to make in our life involves things that are not clearly specified in the Bible. For example, it may involve a certain type of music you like to listen to, some recreational pursuit you enjoy, some types of literature you read, some places you like to go, or some games you like to play. It may also involve things you say about other people when they are not present or attitudes you have toward people who have hurt you or have hurt someone you care about. It is in these areas of life that we find ourselves reluctant to admit that it is really God speaking. Too often we wish to take a "Gallup poll" and ask other Christians if they think a certain practice is wrong or if they think it is really God talking to us. We find ourselves measuring ourselves among ourselves or by what other Christians do or do not do.[10] This problem arises when we are more concerned about being happy or pleasing ourselves than we are about pleasing Jesus in everything.[11]

> **Even after we are saved, self-centeredness continues in our life and causes us spiritual problems**

This internal struggle should alert us to our inherent self-centeredness.[12] Self-centeredness hinders God's work of progressive sanctification—His work of daily transforming us into the image of Christ. It is the reason we need to be entirely sanctified.

---

10 **2 Corinthians 10:12** "For <u>we dare not</u> class ourselves or compare ourselves with those who commend themselves. But they, <u>measuring themselves by themselves, and comparing themselves among themselves, are not wise</u>."
11 **Colossians 1:10** "That you may walk worthy of the Lord, <u>fully pleasing Him</u>, being fruitful in every good work and increasing in the knowledge of God."
12 **Isaiah 53:6** "All we like sheep have gone astray; /<u>We have turned, every one, to his own way</u>; /And the LORD has laid on Him the iniquity of us all."

➡ Because God Has Provided the Grace for Entire Sanctification

God inspired Paul to write that God wishes to sanctify completely every Christian, and that should be enough incentive for any sincere Christian to seek prayerfully this work of God's sovereign grace.

> *1 Thessalonians 5:23, 24: "Now may the God of peace Himself <u>sanctify you completely</u>; and may your whole spirit, soul, and body be preserved blameless at the coming of our Lord Jesus Christ. He who calls you is faithful, who also will do it."*

Let's examine the context and meaning of 1 Thessalonians 5:23, 24, the golden text for entire sanctification.

Paul is writing to genuine Christians. This is established by the fact that they had a faith that worked, a love that labored, and a steadfast hope in Jesus Christ.[13] Their faith and joy served as an example to all the believers in Macedonia and Achaia.[14] They had turned from their idols to serve the living and true God and were expectantly waiting for the second coming of the Lord Jesus Christ.[15] Without a doubt, they were dynamic Christians. But they had not yet been *entirely sanctified*.

The way the Thessalonian Christians recognized their need to be *entirely sanctified* was through Paul's letter. He tells them he is greatly burdened for them. He was praying night and day exceedingly that he would be able to return to them and perfect what was lacking in their faith.[16] The phrase "perfect what is lack-

---

[13] **1 Thessalonians 1:3** "Remembering without ceasing your <u>work of faith</u>, <u>labor of love</u>, and <u>patience of hope</u> in our Lord Jesus Christ in the sight of our God and Father."

[14] **1 Thessalonians 1:7-8** "So that <u>you became examples to all</u> in Macedonia and Achaia who believe. For from you the word of the Lord has sounded forth, not only in Macedonia and Achaia, but also in every place. <u>Your faith toward God has gone out, so that we do not need to say anything.</u>"

[15] **1 Thessalonians 1:9-10** "For they themselves declare concerning us what manner of entry we had to you, and how <u>you turned to God from idols to serve the living and true God</u>, and to <u>wait for His Son from heaven</u>, whom He raised from the dead, even Jesus who delivers us from the wrath to come."

[16] **1 Thessalonians 3:10** "<u>Night and day praying exceedingly</u> that we may see your face and <u>perfect what is lacking in your faith</u>."

ing in your faith" indicates that an essential spiritual ingredient was missing from their lives.[17]

What was missing in their faith? Clearly, it was not something they should have received at conversion, for Paul found no fault with their conversion.[18] But they still needed something more. This implies that it is normal for a newly converted person to have this lack. A person can be thoroughly converted and be a dynamic Christian like the Thessalonians were but still have this need.

> **This work of entire sanctification does not require a long period of time.**

Their faith was not yet complete in two senses. First, they were lacking some important *information* about God's grace and His desire to sanctify them entirely. A person cannot have faith for something that he doesn't know he needs. Paul knew they needed the empowerment of entire sanctification to stand firm in spite of persecution and to enable them to abound in love toward all people.[19] An abounding love toward others would be the means by which God would establish their hearts blameless in holiness (1 Thes. 3:13).[20]

This work of entire sanctification was not something that would require a long period of time. The fact that Paul expected

---

[17] The word *perfect* has the basic idea of to "mend, restore, set right, make complete." In this context it means to "make complete."

[18] They had received the message of salvation as "the word of God, which also effectively works in you who believe" (1 Thessalonians 2:13). The faith necessary for salvation was complete.

[19] Read 1 Thessalonians 3:1-8 for a description of Paul's concern that the Thessalonian believers would maintain their faith in Christ in spite of the tremendous persecution they were experiencing, and 1 Thessalonians 3:12 which speaks of their need to increase and abound in love toward each other and all other people, even as Paul did toward them.

[20] The phrase "so that" (*eis*) at the beginning of 1 Thessalonians 3:13 indicates the ultimate purpose of both Paul's desire to visit them again (3:11) and his prayer for them to abound in love one toward another (3:12). Their hearts needed to be *established blameless* in holiness (sanctification).

this need to be met during his next visit shows that it could be accomplished immediately by faith.

Secondly, their faith was not yet complete because they needed personally to *appropriate* God's work of entire sanctification by faith.[21]

Paul concludes his first letter to the Thessalonians by asserting that there are three reasons why every Christian can and must be entirely sanctified. When he says, "He who calls you is faithful, who also will do it" (5:24), Paul is declaring that: 1) God is *calling* all Christians to be entirely sanctified; 2) God's call rests upon His faithful *character*; and 3) God *promises* to sanctify entirely every Christian who appropriates by faith His provision—"He will do it."

> **God is *calling* all Christians to be entirely sanctified.**

"How *entire* or *complete* is entire sanctification?" Is Paul implying that there will be no further progress in sanctification? No. When he uses the adverb *entirely*, he is speaking of a work of God's sanctifying grace that purifies *every part of man*: "spirit, soul, and body."[22]

The phrase, "May your whole spirit, soul, and body be preserved blameless at the coming of our Lord Jesus Christ" (5:23b), indicates that God desires to sanctify you entirely and "preserve" you in this grace until Jesus comes back for His Church. The word *preserve* means "to maintain, to be kept or preserved." The grace of God can *entirely sanctify* (cleanse and purify every part of you)

---

21 When Paul prays that they might be *sanctified completely* or *entirely*, two important truths are communicated. First, it is God's will that all Christians be entirely sanctified. Thus, it is essential and indispensable. Second, it is God's work, rather than man's work, that produces entire sanctification.

22 In this context, the word *spirit* refers to the inner chamber of your being—your heart—the control panel out of which your thoughts and motives proceed. The word *soul* includes your mind, will, and emotions. These must be cleansed of self-centeredness and consecrated for God's glory. The word *body* refers to the physical, material, fleshly part of man that is to be used only for God's honor and glory, in harmony with His word.

and keep you entirely sanctified until Jesus returns.[23] "He who calls you is faithful, who also will do it" (5:24).

What Is Involved in Entire Sanctification?

Entire sanctification is a purifying of the heart and a strengthening of the personal relationship we have with God through Jesus Christ. This relationship—the gift of eternal life[24]—was initiated at our new birth.[25]

In entire sanctification, the heart is purified when we present ourselves to God as a living sacrifice,[26] yielding ourselves to the controlling presence of the Holy Spirit.[27] When we exercise faith in His word, God delivers us from our self-centeredness.[28] As a result, our relationship with God is strengthened and we are fur-

---

23 It is important to understand that entire sanctification is available to all Christians immediately upon their full surrender and faith. Do not misunderstand the meaning of the phrase, "at the coming of our Lord Jesus Christ." There are three reasons we know that Paul is not saying believers have to wait until Jesus returns to be completely sanctified. 1) First, it fails to account for Paul's great prayer burden for the Thessalonian believers. If entire sanctification is the result of a gradual process, and if all believers who walk in the light will gradually attain unto it, and if it cannot be completed until Jesus returns, there was no reason for Paul to be so burdened for them. 2) Second, it fails to take into account the phrase, "be preserved blameless." You cannot be preserved blameless in holiness unless you are entirely sanctified. That entire sanctification is obtainable in this life by faith is implied in the verb translated "preserved." The grace of God that can sanctify you completely, spirit, soul, and body, can keep you entirely sanctified. 3) Third, the preposition "at" (*en*) can be translated many ways. In this context, it would be best to translate it "unto." Entire sanctification is to be accomplished in preparation for the second coming of the Lord.
24 **John 17:3** "And this is eternal life, that they may know You, the only true God, and Jesus Christ whom You have sent."
25 **Romans 6:23** "For the wages of sin is death, but the gift of God is eternal life in Christ Jesus our Lord."
26 **Romans 12:1** "I beseech you therefore, brethren, by the mercies of God, that you present your bodies a living sacrifice, holy, acceptable to God, which is your reasonable service."
27 The phrase "controlling presence of the Holy Spirit" is not speaking of "making" a Christian do something contrary to his will (there is nothing coercive about the Holy Spirit). Rather, it speaks of a willing, moment-by-moment surrender and obedience to whatever changes the Spirit wishes to make in the Christian's life.
28 The sense in which we are cleansed of self-centeredness can be understood by the following analogy: consider a piece of thin plastic pipe that has a kink or bend. The bend is symbolic of our self-centeredness. In order to straighten the pipe, we can run hot water through it to soften it and allow gravity to pull the bend out of the pipe. The hot water and gravity are symbolic of the cleansing power and influence of the Holy Spirit in our lives. Daily yielding to the Spirit's control allows us to be free from the inner bent to sin and remain submissive to God. However, if we resist the Spirit and rebel against His control—effectively stopping the hot water from running through the pipe—we will find ourselves back to self-centered living.

ther empowered to grow in Christlikeness and to serve Him more effectively.

Just as God desires all sinners to be saved, so God desires all Christians to be entirely sanctified.[29]

I Believe . . .
Entire sanctification is a specific work of God's grace by which He cleanses the Christian's heart from inherited depravity and fills him with the Holy Spirit. This cleansing enables the Christian to love God completely and his neighbor as himself unhindered by self-centeredness. It also strengthens his relationship with God, thereby empowering him to be a witness and to serve God more effectively.

Questions for Study

1. What is the Scripture passage from which the term entire sanctification is derived?

2. What are the three ways in which sanctification is used in Scripture?

3. What is initial sanctification?

4. What is progressive sanctification?

5. What is entire sanctification?

6. Why do we need to be entirely sanctified?

7. How does entire sanctification affect your relationship with God?

---

[29] 1 Thessalonians 5:23.

Recommended Reading

Oswalt, John N. *Called to Be Holy*. Nappanee, IN: Evangel Publishing House, 1999.

Taylor, Richard S. *Exploring Christian Holiness*. Vol. 3. Kansas City: Beacon Hill Press, 1985.
See especially chapter 9, "Experiencing Heart Holiness," pp. 167-186.

13

Steps to Entire Sanctification

It is God's desire to entirely sanctify every Christian, and He has designed a way for every believer to experience that grace. Let's talk about how a Christian can seek and experience entire sanctification.

First let's review the definition of entire sanctification.

Entire sanctification is a specific work of God's grace by which He cleanses the Christian's heart from inherited depravity and fills him with the Holy Spirit. This cleansing enables him to love God completely and his neighbor as himself, unhindered by self-centeredness.[1] It also strengthens his relationship with God, thereby empowering him to serve God more effectively.

Now let's examine how to be entirely sanctified.

Step 1: Recognize and Admit Your Need to Be Entirely Sanctified.

There are at least two ways a Christian can recognize his need to be entirely sanctified.

➡ First, every Christian eventually becomes aware of his remaining self-centeredness. He begins to realize that he has an inner sinfulness of heart that takes the form of pride and selfishness. He also may find himself resisting the work of the Holy Spirit, who is guiding him to make changes in his actions and attitudes to make him pleasing to God and a better example of a person transformed by God's grace.

---

1 Because self-centeredness appears to be the primary manifestation of our corrupt nature, I use the phrase self-centeredness as short hand for inherited depravity throughout this chapter.

> The second is simply by believing the testimony of Scripture. God promises to entirely sanctify the believer.[2]

A Christian will not seriously desire and seek to be entirely sanctified until he realizes his need.

Step 2: In Prayer, Present Yourself to God as a Living Sacrifice, Yielding Yourself to the Control of the Holy Spirit.

Paul tells us in Romans 12:1, "I beseech you therefore, brethren, by the mercies of God, that ye present your bodies a living sacrifice, holy, acceptable unto God, which is your reasonable service."[3]

As Christians, they are to present their "bodies a living sacrifice, holy, acceptable unto God." The Greek word *present* is translated in Romans 6:13 and 6:19 as *yield*. The basic idea of *present* or *yield* in this context is to put yourself at the disposal of God, to renounce your rights and preferences and tell God you are turning everything connected with your life over to Him. This is a deliberate act of full surrender to God.[4] It could also be called total consecration.

---

[2] For fuller discussion of the ways in which a person can realize his need for entire sanctification, see Chapter 12.

[3] Paul is writing to Christians. In Romans 1:7 he calls them "saints"—holy people. In Romans 1:8 he says their "faith is spoken of throughout the whole world." In Romans 16:19 he praises them that their obedience to Christ is known to all. They are genuine believers who are presently serving God faithfully. Romans 12:1 is therefore addressed to people who are already born again.

[4] Sometimes Christians say they made a full surrender to God when they were saved. It is true that there is a surrender involved in getting saved, but it is a different kind of surrender. The surrender you made to God when you repented of your sins and asked Him to forgive you was the surrender a rebel makes when he lays down his weapons in submission to the conquering general. As a sinner, you were spiritually dead in trespasses and sin (Eph. 2:1). Nothing about you before you were saved was holy or acceptable to God (Isa. 64:6). When you repented of your sins and exercised faith to believe, God forgave you and made you a new creation in Christ Jesus (2 Cor. 5:17). He imparted to you "newness of life" (Rom. 6:4), and you were made spiritually alive and holy to God. But Romans 12:1 is not addressed to sinners. It is addressed to Christians—to people who are spiritually alive ("living") and holy. It is a call to a different kind of surrender. Christians are asked to surrender their bodies to God as a living sacrifice. God is asking Christians to turn over to Him the complete control of their lives now that they are in a right relationship with God.

The motivation for Christians to present their bodies a living sacrifice is the "mercies of God." In light of God's saving, forgiving mercy, the proper response for any Christian is willing and prompt obedience. God asks us to yield ourselves to Him with the understanding that we are deliberately renouncing all rights to our own desires, opinions, and choices. We are asked to surrender unconditionally to God's will and purposes for our life, fully transferring control to Him for all time.

When a Christian offers himself as "a living sacrifice, holy, acceptable to God," he is doing only what is his "reasonable service," or "reasonable act of worship." A Christian should gladly offer himself in a full, conscious, moment-by-moment surrender to God as a thankful response for His saving grace.

To present yourself as a living sacrifice means that you completely yield yourself to the control of the Holy Spirit. This truth is taught in Ephesians 5:18, where Paul commands, "Be filled with the Spirit."

Every Christian, from the moment of the new birth, receives the Holy Spirit into his life and is *indwelt* by the Holy Spirit.[5] However, when a Christian is *filled* with the Spirit, the Spirit is invited to take *full control* of every aspect of the believer's life. To be filled with the Spirit does not mean you receive more of the Spirit. It means that the Holy Spirit is given full control over every aspect of your life. Without any reservation you fully surrender control to the Holy Spirit. You thereby acknowledge His right to change anything or everything about you whenever He wishes!

> **Every Christian, from the moment of the new birth, receives the Holy Spirit into his life.**

---

5   **1 Corinthians 2:12; 6:19; Galatians 4:6; Romans 8:9-11**. There is a difference between being "indwelt" (*oikeo, enoikeo*) by the Spirit and being "filled" (*pleroo*) with the Spirit. Every Christian, from the moment of the new birth, receives the Holy Spirit into his life and is indwelt by the Holy Spirit, but he is not filled with the Spirit. Paul is commanding Christians who are indwelt by the Spirit to be filled and/or remain filled with the Spirit. The filling with the Spirit is therefore subsequent to the new birth.

Perhaps the analogy of driving a car can illustrate how being filled with the Spirit is to impact our daily lives. The Holy Spirit desires to control the direction and speed of the car (which represents our life). Some of us would like to remove ourselves from the driver's seat, and let the Holy Spirit drive. That would eliminate the stress of decision making. It would let us take a passive role. Instead, the Holy Spirit insists that we stay in the driver's seat. He is going to ride with us, but is going to tell us what to do. So He issues instructions (through Scripture and in the form of prompts and checks), and we, as the driver, are to submit to His control moment-by-moment.

This illustration emphasizes that the fullness of the Spirit is not a simplistic "let go and let God have His way," one-time decision that becomes automatic from that point forward. A person who has fully surrendered to the control of the Holy Spirit demonstrates this surrender through moment-by-moment obedience. As he lives under the Spirit's control in moment-by-moment obedience, he is continually kept clean from the former corruption of his nature that would make him self-centered and inclined to sin.

Step 3: Pray in Faith for God's Work of Entire Sanctification.

So far, we have seen that in order to be entirely sanctified, God asks the believer to present himself to God as a living sacrifice,[6] thereby surrendering full control of his life to the Holy Spirit.[7] We now come to the crucial element of faith. Just as God expects the sinner to receive His gift of forgiveness by faith in the finished work of Jesus Christ, God expects the Christian to receive His provision of entire sanctification by faith.

What is biblical faith? According to Hebrews 11:6 biblical faith has three aspects:

1) You must believe what God says ("He *is* a rewarder of those who diligently seek Him");

---
[6] Romans 12:1.
[7] Ephesians 5:18.

2) You must commit to do what God requires ("diligently seek Him");

3) You must trust in and rest on what God promises ("He is a rewarder of those who diligently seek Him").[8]

Questions for Personal Application

Ask yourself the following questions:

→ As a born again Christian, am I walking in all the light I now have?[9] If you are not, ask God to forgive you and begin walking in all the light God has given you. If you are presently walking in all the light God has given you, consider the next questions.

→ Have I obeyed Romans 12:1 and presented my body to God as a living sacrifice, holy, acceptable to God, which is my reasonable service? Have I consciously, deliberately, fully, surrendered everything I am and have to God—my past, my present, my future, my dreams and ambitions, my relationships, everything I can think of now, and have I willingly committed myself to maintain a full surrender to the will of God concerning anything that may come up in the future?

→ Have I obeyed Ephesians 5:18 and asked God to fill me with His Spirit? Do I understand that to be filled with the Spirit I must surrender full control of my life to the Spirit? Have I surrendered to God my "rights" to life, liberty, and the pursuit of happiness? Have I purposed to do, to the best of my ability, whatever God tells me to do, without reservations or retreat? Have I responded with obedience and consecration in every area that God has shown to me as I have been seeking in prayer?

---

8   For more on biblical faith, see chapter 14: "Three Pillars of Assurance."
9   **1 John 1:7**: "If we walk in the light as He is in the light, we have fellowship with one another, and the blood of Jesus Christ His Son cleanses us from all sin." Walking in the light is required by God in order to maintain your relationship with Jesus. If you are not walking in the light, you are committing willful sin, and no one who has willful sin in his life will enter heaven (Matthew 7:21-23).

If you can say without doubt or reservation, "With the help of God, Yes," to the above questions, then have you taken the next step and in prayer received God's gift of entire sanctification by faith? Have you fully completed all three aspects of biblical faith? Are you presently trusting in and <u>resting on</u> what God promises? He promises to sanctify completely any Christian who makes a full, unconditional surrender of himself to God and turns over full control of his life to the Holy Spirit.

If you can say "Yes" to all of these questions without reservation, you have the biblical right to believe and testify to others that God has sanctified you wholly.[10] Paul says there is peace and joy in believing.[11] And the Apostle John assures us, "Now this is the confidence that we have in Him, that if we ask anything according to His will, He hears us. And if we know that He hears us, whatever we ask, we know that *we have the petitions that we have asked of Him.*"[12] From this point on, make sure you keep your commitment to God and stay fully surrendered.

What Changes Can I Expect in My Life after I Am Entirely Sanctified?

There are many changes that occur after a person is entirely sanctified. We cannot explore all the changes in this chapter, but let me emphasize an important change. You can expect a new ability to fulfill the two great commandments. By God's grace, you will now be able to love God with all your heart, with all your soul, and with all your mind, and your neighbor as yourself.[13]

This is what Paul is referring to when he speaks of an entirely sanctified Christian being "preserved blameless in the eyes of

---

10 For more about the "witness of the Spirit," see the chapter entitled, "The Three Pillars of Assurance."
11 **Romans 15:13** "Now may the God of hope <u>fill you with all joy and peace in believing</u>, that you may abound in hope by the power of the Holy Spirit."
12 1 John 5:14, 15.
13 **Matthew 22:36-40** "'Teacher, which is the great commandment in the law?' Jesus said to him, 'You shall love the LORD your God with all your heart, with all your soul, and with all your mind. This is the first and great commandment. And the second is like it: You shall love your neighbor as yourself. On these two commandments hang all the Law and the Prophets.'"

God."[14] The focus of blamelessness is on how God views our motives and our treatment of other people. God preserves an entirely sanctified person *blameless in holiness* by enabling him to love others whole-heartedly and maintain blameless interpersonal relationships.[15] Therefore, entire sanctification is characterized not only by the cleansing of our lives from self-centeredness and the full control of the Holy Spirit, but also by the impartation of grace that enables us to "increase and abound in love" toward everyone.[16] Paul demonstrated this type of abounding love to the Thessalonians ("just as we do to you").

> **You can expect a new ability to fulfill the two great commandments.**

God wants you to learn how to demonstrate your love for Him and others by loving what God loves.[17] For example, God loves sinners and actively seeks to save them.[18] Therefore the entirely sanctified Christian will also love sinners and become more actively engaged in seeking their salvation. In the Book of Acts, when Christians were filled with the Spirit (*entirely* sanctified), they became more evangelistic than they had been before.[19] You will love all sinners, not just your lost family and friends, but also your neighbors, your co-workers, the people at the store, your enemies—in short, all people who do not know Jesus Christ as their Savior.

---

14 **1 Thessalonians 5:23b** "…and may your whole spirit, soul, and body be preserved blameless at the coming of our Lord Jesus Christ."
15 By "blameless" we do not mean that a person is faultless. He will make mistakes that affect his relationships with others, but he is "blameless" in the sense that he does what he sincerely thinks is consistent with love.
16 **1 Thessalonians 3:12** "And may the Lord make you increase and abound in love to one another and to all, just as we *do* to you."
17 **John 14:15** "If you love Me, keep My commandments."
18 **John 3:16** "For God so loved the world that He gave His only begotten Son, that whoever believes in Him should not perish but have everlasting life."
19 **Acts 1:8** "But you shall receive power when the Holy Spirit has come upon you; and you shall be witnesses to Me in Jerusalem, and in all Judea and Samaria, and to the end of the earth."

A Prayer for Entire Sanctification

Dear Heavenly Father, I come to you in Jesus' name. I thank you for saving me and making me your child. I know that all my sins have been washed away through the precious blood of Jesus. I also thank you for the assurance that if I ask anything in harmony with your will for my life, you hear me. You tell me in 1 John 5:14, 15 that if you hear me, then I know that I have what I am asking for. Thank you for this wonderful promise.

I come as your child to place myself without reservation on your altar as a living sacrifice for time and eternity. I fully surrender to you my body, my dreams, my wishes, my friends, my past, my present, my future, all I have. I ask you to cleanse my heart. With your help, I yield full control of my life to you. All that I have is yours forever. Entirely sanctify my heart just now. Please enable me to love you and to love my neighbor as myself free from self-centeredness.

Father, thank you for providing the means for my entire sanctification through the blood of Jesus. Holy Spirit, come now in your fullness and entirely sanctify my heart. I trust you to be faithful to do it just now. I pray this prayer of full consecration and surrender in the precious name of Jesus, and by faith receive your promise.

I praise you, Father, for you have willed this work of entire sanctification. I praise you, Lord Jesus, for you shed your blood that I might be entirely sanctified. I praise you, Holy Spirit, for doing this wonderful work of grace in my heart! Amen and amen.

A Closing Word of Encouragement

Romans 10:8-13 teaches the importance of confessing with our mouth what we believe with our heart. It is important that you share with others what God has done for you. Do not be afraid. God blesses those who obey Him.

I Believe . . .
God is faithful to entirely sanctify the Christian when he presents himself to God as a living sacrifice, surrenders himself to the control of the Holy Spirit, and in faith receives the promised sanctifying grace.

Questions for Study

1. What are two ways a Christian can recognize his need to be entirely sanctified?

2. What does the adverb "entirely" mean in the verse from which we infer the phrase, "entire sanctification"?

3. Review the four personal, searching questions at the conclusion of the chapter. Consider them not merely as doctrinal points, but as personal questions.

Recommended Reading:

Drury, Keith. *Holiness for Ordinary People*. Indianapolis: Wesleyan Publishing House, 2004. See chapter 1, pp. 13-25.

Taylor, Richard S., ed. *Exploring Christian Holiness*. Vol. 3. Kansas City: Beacon Hill Press, 1985. See chapter 9, "Experiencing Heart Holiness," pp. 167-186.

14

The Three Pillars of Assurance

If you are like many Christians, you have asked someone you trust, "How can I know for sure that I am saved?" or "What evidence should I look for to know that I am entirely sanctified?" These questions are intensely personal and practical for someone who has doubts about his spiritual condition.

Though you may have struggled with doubts, the Bible tells us that we can live in confidence of God's acceptance. God's Spirit assures us that we are adopted children of God and do not need to live in fear.[1] This assurance is so complete that we can have boldness in the day of judgment. We do not have to wonder whether or not we will pass God's evaluation.[2]

There are at least three means of assurance described in Scripture. God uses all three of these means to assure us of our acceptance with Him. The three means of assurance described in the Bible are: (1) the assurance of faith in God's word, (2) the witness of the Spirit, and (3) the assurance of obedience.

The Assurance of Faith in God's Word

When we meet the conditions of a promise from God, the promise itself brings to us assurance. But the testimony of Scripture brings assurance only when we have biblical faith.

---

[1] **Romans 8:14-16** "For as many as are led by the Spirit of God, these are sons of God. For you did not receive the spirit of bondage again to fear, but you received the Spirit of adoption by whom we cry out, 'Abba, Father.' The Spirit Himself bears witness with our spirit that we are children of God."

[2] **1 John 4:17** "Love has been perfected among us in this: that we may have boldness in the day of judgment; because as He is, so are we in this world."

Hebrews 11:6 helps us with a description of what true biblical faith is:

1) You must believe what God says (believe that "He <u>is</u> a rewarder of those who diligently seek Him");

2) You must commit to do what God requires (you must "<u>diligently</u> seek Him");

3) You must trust in and rest on what God promises (rest in Him as the "<u>rewarder</u> of those who diligently seek Him").

➡ **Faith believes what God says.**

The first element of faith is believing that God has communicated His will for mankind in the Bible. Faith believes all that the Bible says is true. To the repentant sinner God says, "If we confess our sins, He is faithful and just to forgive us our sins, and to cleanse us from all unrighteousness."[3] "The one who comes to me I will by no means cast out."[4] "Come now, and let us reason together, says the LORD: though your sins be as scarlet, they shall be as white as snow; though they be red like crimson, they shall be as wool."[5] "Repent therefore and be converted, that your sins may be blotted out."[6] Faith requires that you believe what God says.

The element of believing what God says also applies to commands and inspired prayers. For example, God commands Christians, "Be filled with the Spirit."[7] He says to all Christians, "I beseech you therefore, brethren, by the mercies of God, that you present your bodies a living sacrifice, holy, acceptable to God, which is your reasonable service."[8] It is God's will that all Chris-

---

[3] 1 John 1:9.
[4] **John 6:37** "All that the Father gives Me will come to Me, and <u>the one who comes to Me I will by no means cast out</u>."
[5] **Isaiah 1:18** "'Come now, and let us reason together,' says the LORD, 'Though your sins are like scarlet, /They shall be as white as snow; /Though they are red like crimson, /They shall be as wool.'"
[6] **Acts 3:19** "Repent therefore and be converted, that your sins may be blotted out, so that times of refreshing may come from the presence of the Lord"
[7] **Ephesians 5:18** "And do not be drunk with wine, in which is dissipation; but <u>be filled with the Spirit</u>."
[8] Romans 12:1.

tians be entirely sanctified now and be preserved in that cleansed and empowered relationship until Jesus returns. God inspired Paul to pray for the Thessalonians: "Now may the God of peace Himself sanctify you completely; and may your whole spirit, soul, and body be preserved blameless at the coming of our Lord Jesus Christ. He who calls you is faithful, who also will do it."[9] God wants to entirely sanctify all Christians. Biblical faith means that you believe what God says about what He wants to do in your life.

➡ **Faith commits to do what God requires.**

The second element of faith is that you commit to do what God requires. For the sinner to do what God requires means that he must confess his sins in true repentance. Repentance is motivated by godly sorrow which produces a change of heart, mind, and attitude toward sin and ungodliness, and is demonstrated by a change in attitude and behavior.[10] In other words, true repentance requires you to stop all that you know is wrong, and begin to do all you know is right. Without a change of attitude and behavior, there has been no biblical repentance. Have you thoroughly repented of all your sins?

> **Without a change of attitude and behavior, there has been no biblical repentance.**

For the Christian seeking entire sanctification, the second element of faith means that he will do what God commands. Have you made an unconditional surrender to God of your body?[11] Have you turned full control of every aspect of your life and existence over to the Holy Spirit?[12] Have you asked God to

---

9 1 Thessalonians 5:23, 24.
10 **2 Corinthians 7:10** "For <u>godly sorrow produces repentance leading to salvation, not to be regretted</u>; but the sorrow of the world produces death."
11 **Romans 12:1** "I beseech you therefore, brethren, by the mercies of God, that <u>you present your bodies a living sacrifice</u>, holy, acceptable to God, which is your reasonable service."
12 **Ephesians 5:18** "And do not be drunk with wine, in which is dissipation; but <u>be filled with the Spirit</u>."

sanctify you entirely?[13] If not, you are not doing what the Bible requires, and therefore you are not exercising biblical faith.

> **Faith trusts in and rests on what God promises.**

The third element of faith is trusting in and resting on what God promises. This is perhaps the hardest of the three elements of biblical faith. We are to trust in and rest on what God says because of the character of God. He cannot lie.[14] He will never fail. Nothing can keep Him from fulfilling His promise, if you have met the conditions of the promise. Faith means that we *trust in* what He has promised because God is worthy of our trust, and faith means that we *rest on* what He has promised, because He always does what He promises.

It is at this point that most people have a faith battle. Until you have settled it in your heart and mind that God is fully trustworthy and always does what He promises, you will not be able to rest in His promises. If you are still trying to trust God, or trying to rest in His promises and believe He has done what you asked, you do not yet have complete faith. You must get beyond the trying stage. Through the enabling help of the Spirit, you can get to the point of full confidence in God's promise. When your faith is complete, you can say with utmost confidence and assurance, "I am resting in the promises of God and thereby am confident He has done what He promised to do."

The act of resting on what God promised does bring a *feeling*. You know when you are at rest, and that is a very different feeling from anxiety, or being unsure, or simply hoping that God did for you what He promised He would do. Paul tells us that joy and peace are the fruits of biblical faith: "Now may the God of hope fill you with all joy and peace in believing . . ." (Romans 15:13).

The act of trusting in and resting on the promises of God is the way to have what the Apostle John calls the witness (or assur-

---

[13] **1 Thessalonians 5:23-24** "Now may the God of peace Himself sanctify you completely; and may your whole spirit, soul, and body be preserved blameless at the coming of our Lord Jesus Christ. He who calls you is faithful, who also will do it."
[14] **Titus 1:2** "In hope of eternal life which God, who cannot lie, promised before time began."

ance) in us.[15] Read the following Scripture carefully. I have underlined key phrases to which you should pay special attention. Notice that when you truly believe God's witness to us through His word, you receive an internal witness (assurance) from God. This is an inner rest of mind and heart that comes from believing that God has done for you what He promised He would do.

> If we receive the witness of men, <u>the witness of God</u> is greater; for <u>this is the witness of God</u> which He has testified of His Son. <u>He who believes</u> in the Son of God <u>has the witness in himself</u>; he who does not believe God has made Him a liar, because he has <u>not believed the testimony</u> that God has given of His Son. And this is the testimony: that God has given us eternal life, and this life is in His Son. He who has the Son has life; he who does not have the Son of God does not have life. <u>These things I have written to you</u> who believe in the name of the Son of God, <u>that you may know that you have eternal life</u>, and that you may continue to believe in the name of the Son of God. Now this is <u>the confidence</u> that we have in Him, that if we ask anything according to His will, He hears us. And if we know that He hears us, whatever we ask, <u>we know</u> that we have the petitions that we have asked of Him (1 John 5:9-15).

The primary way a person gains assurance that God has either saved him or entirely sanctified him is by faith in God's word. Faith believes that God is able to perform what He has promised in Holy Scripture. Faith is the conviction and assurance that God is able and willing to do what He promised *now* (if the conditions of the promise have been met), and it is the

> **Faith rests in a sure confidence that God does now fulfill His promise.**

conviction and assurance that He indeed *does it now*. Faith rests in a sure confidence that God does now fulfill His promise because He always does what He says He will do. You are not exercising

---

[15] **1 John 5:10** "<u>He who believes</u> in the Son of God <u>has the witness in himself</u>; he who does not believe God has made Him a liar, because he has not believed <u>the testimony</u> that God has given of His Son."

faith if you are waiting for a special emotion in order to trust God. You must securely rest in the fact that, if you have met the conditions of God's promise, He has done what He promised.

Lest it sound like I am talking about a simple "name it and claim it" methodology or "easy believism," I wish to give a word of warning. If there is no change of life that follows and backs up your claim to having received God's saving grace by faith or your claim to having received God's work of entire sanctification by faith, then your faith is not a biblical faith. There is always the visible evidence of the fruit of the Spirit and the fruit of obedience in the life of the person who has exercised biblical faith. We'll talk about this "third pillar" of assurance a little later.

The Witness of the Spirit

The Bible also speaks of an assurance that comes to us by the Holy Spirit apart from Scripture—a divinely imparted inner consciousness that God has saved us ("The Spirit Himself bears witness with our spirit that we are the children of God"),[16] or that God has entirely sanctified us, and that we are pleasing Him. This direct witness of the Spirit is not always perceived immediately upon conversion or at the moment of entire sanctification. But sooner or later, the Holy Spirit will witness to our hearts that He has accomplished His work of grace.

John Wesley taught that the witness of the Spirit is the privilege of every believer. True Christians should expect at some point a direct witness from God that they are saved (or entirely sanctified if that is what they are trusting God for). Wesley defined the witness of the Spirit for salvation as: "The inward impression of the soul, whereby the Spirit of God immediately and directly witnesses to my spirit that I am a child of God; that Jesus Christ hath loved me, and given Himself for me; that all my sins are blotted out, and I, even I, am reconciled to God."[17]

---

[16] Romans 8:16.
[17] *Works:* "Witness of the Spirit," 5:124-25.

The universal testimony of the church is that the awareness of this direct witness of the Spirit is not an abiding, always present, conscious perception. Sometimes it is very clear, and at other times, especially during times of sickness or Satanic oppression, it is not discernable at all. Further, one cannot dictate to God the timing of the witness nor the form in which this direct assurance comes.

John Wesley tells the mistake he and his fellow Methodist ministers made during the early years of their preaching on the importance of the witness of the Spirit for assurance for salvation. Speaking of his ministers he wrote, "They were apt to make sad the hearts of those whom God had not made sad. For they frequently asked those who feared God, 'Do you know that your sins are forgiven?' [In other words, do you have a direct witness of the Holy Spirit that you are forgiven]. And upon their answering, 'No,' immediately replied, 'Then you are a child of the devil.' 'No; that does not follow.'"[18] John Wesley explained that they had not clearly understood that whoever fears God and works righteousness is accepted of God.[19] Therefore, he would affirm the progress the believer had made and tell them to keep walking in the light and not to doubt God. He assured them that they were no longer under the wrath of God and that sooner or later they would receive the direct witness of the Spirit.

> Sooner or later, the Holy Spirit will witness to our hearts that He has accomplished His work of grace.

Because of the variableness of one's perception of the witness of the Spirit, this means of assurance, although thoroughly Scriptural and important, is not to be our primary basis of assurance. If it

---

18 John Wesley, "On Faith," in *The Sermons of Wesley*, Sermon 106, p. 218.
19 **Acts 10:35** "But in every nation whoever fears Him and works righteousness is accepted by Him."

were, a person would lack assurance whenever he could not sense the direct witness of the Spirit. Paul makes it clear in Romans 1:17 that the just shall live by faith. The assurance that comes from believing God's word is the stabilizing, constant, abiding basis for assurance.[20]

The Assurance of Obedience

Scripture speaks of a third means of assurance that God has done a specific, personal work of grace. In addition to the assurance of faith in God's word, and the assurance through our inner perception of the Holy Spirit's approval, there is the assurance that comes through obedience to God's word. The First Epistle of John majors on this kind of assurance. Through measurable attitudes and actions, we can examine ourselves to see if we are truly in the faith.

Read the following verses from 1 John. We are offered assurance that we are right with God when specific, measurable attitudes and actions are true about us. Pay special attention to verses that tell us how we "know" that we know God, that we are in a right relationship with Him.

- **Measurable action:** We are not to walk in darkness—willfully practice known sin. "If we say that we have fellowship with Him, and walk in darkness, we lie and do not practice the truth" (1 John 1:6).

- **Measurable action:** We are to walk in the light—obey what we know. "But if we walk in the light as He is in the light, we have fellowship with one another, and the blood of Jesus Christ His Son cleanses us from all sin" (1 John 1:7).

- **Measurable action:** Assurance comes by obeying God's commandments. "Now by this *we know that we know Him*, if we keep His commandments. He who says, 'I know Him,'

---

[20] Richard S. Taylor, *Exploring Christian Holiness*, Vol. 3, *The Theological Formulation*, (Kansas City: Beacon Hill Press, 1985), 181. Taylor writes, "Neither can the emphasis on the Word of God as the true ground of assurance be challenged."

and does not keep His commandments, is a liar, and the truth is not in him. But whoever keeps His word, truly the love of God is perfected in him. *By this we know that we are in Him*" (1 John 2:3-5).

- **Measurable attitude:** A person who hates another person is not a Christian. "He who says he is in the light, and hates his brother, is in darkness until now" (1 John 2:9).

- **Measurable action:** A person who practices righteousness is a Christian. "If *you know* that He is righteous, you know that everyone who practices righteousness is born of Him" (1 John 2:29).

- **Measurable action:** A person who practices willful sin is not a Christian. "He who sins is of the devil, for the devil has sinned from the beginning. For this purpose the Son of God was manifested, that He might destroy the works of the devil. Whoever has been born of God does not sin, for His seed remains in him; and he cannot sin, because he has been born of God. In this the children of God and the children of the devil are manifest: Whoever does not practice righteousness is not of God, nor is he who does not love his brother" (1 John 3:8-10).

- **Measurable attitude:** A Christian loves everyone and hates no one. "*We know* that we have passed from death to life, because we love the brethren. He who does not love his brother abides in death. Whoever hates his brother is a murderer, and you know that no murderer has eternal life abiding in him" (1 John 3:14-15).

- **Measurable attitude and action:** A Christian is compassionate and helps those who are in genuine need. "By this *we know* love, because He laid down His life for us. And we also ought to lay down our lives for the brethren. But whoever has this world's goods, and sees his brother in need, and shuts up his heart from him, how does the love of God abide in him? My little children, let us not love in word or in tongue, but in deed and in truth. And *by this we know that we are of the truth*, and shall assure our hearts before Him" (1 John 3:16-19).

- **Measurable action:** A Christian keeps God's commandments through the power of the Spirit whom God has given us. "Now he who keeps His commandments abides in Him, and He in him" (1 John 3:24a).

- **Measurable attitude:** A Christian loves all people. "Beloved, let us love one another, for love is of God; and everyone who loves is born of God and *knows God*. He who does not love *does not know God*, for God is love" (1 John 4:7-8).

- **Measurable attitude:** The presence of God's Spirit in us enables us to love all people. "No one has seen God at any time. If we love one another, God abides in us, and His love has been perfected in us. By this *we know* that we abide in Him, and He in us, because He has given us of His Spirit" (1 John 4:12-13).

- **Measurable attitude:** A person who hates another person is not a Christian. "If someone says, 'I love God,' and hates his brother, he is a liar; for he who does not love his brother whom he has seen, how can he love God whom he has not seen? And this commandment we have from Him: that he who loves God must love his brother also" (1 John 4:20-21).

- **Measurable action:** A Christian believes Jesus is the promised Messiah and keeps God's commandments. "Whoever believes that Jesus is the Christ is born of God, and everyone who loves Him who begot also loves him who is begotten of Him. *By this we know* that we love the children of God, when we love God and keep His commandments" (1 John 5:1-2).

As you read through these measurable attitudes and actions, did you notice how frequently John used the term *know*? He was vitally concerned that believers have objective, measurable assurance that they were right with God. One of the ways a person "knows that he knows," according to John, is by the measurable attitudes and actions present in his life. For example, if a person has been harboring ill-will or bitterness in his heart toward someone and if he has refused to forgive the offender, according to John, the person who will not forgive is not a Christian. One of the proofs of being saved is your love towards all other people. Refusing to forgive is not an act of love.

Being born again will result in measurable changes in attitude and action. Being entirely sanctified will also result in measurable changes in attitude and action. A change of disposition and attitude always accompanies the work of entire sanctification.[21] Prior to entire sanctification, the Christian struggles with a divided mind: he wants to please God, but he also wants to please himself. After entire sanctification, there is now one dominating desire in his heart—wholly to love and please Jesus. His consuming passion is to be holy, like Jesus. This has an impact on the way he lives. Whether God saves or entirely sanctifies us, there is a corresponding change in our disposition and actions. This is the assurance of obedience.

Conclusion

What is the biblical basis for assurance? How can we know for sure that we are saved or entirely sanctified? The first means of assurance is faith in God's word. A second means is the direct witness of the Spirit, an inner consciousness God gives to us that He has saved or entirely sanctified us. A third means is the assurance of obedience to God's word. We are to check our attitudes and actions to see if they align with God's word.

---

21 Richard S. Taylor, *Exploring Christian Holiness*, Vol. 3, *The Theological Formulation*, (Kansas City: Beacon Hill Press, 1985), 184-186.

> **I Believe . . . .**
> The Bible promises me that I can know my spiritual condition and be assured that I am pleasing God. The Bible describes three reliable means of assurance: the assurance of faith in God's word, the witness of the Spirit, and the witness of obedience. By these I can know if I am saved and if I am entirely sanctified.

Questions for Study

1. Of what can we be assured?
2. What is the first and most fundamental means of assurance?
3. What are the three elements of biblical faith?
4. What is the second means of assurance discussed?
5. Why should the second means not be our primary basis of assurance?
6. What does it mean that the witness of obedience is a means of assurance?

Recommended Reading:

Keene, S. A. *Heart Talks on Faith*. Salem, OH: Schmul Publishing Co., Rpt. 1986. See chapters 1-5, pp. 9-68.

Taylor, Richard S. *Exploring Christian Holiness*. Vol. 3. Kansas City: Beacon Hill Press, 1985. See chapter 9, "Experiencing Heart Holiness," pp. 167-186.

15

The Church: The Home Where We Belong

"Home is where the heart is." This old motto used to hang in parlors everywhere, and its message remains as true as ever. In all of us is a deep desire for home and family, where by birth and blood we belong. There we live in a community of heritage and love, where children are nurtured, youth are trained, and the elderly are cherished. God intended all this, of course, for it was He who set us in families; and it was He who established our first home in Eden. Yes, at home, we all belong.

This is also true of our spiritual home, which is the church. For the church is God's family, where by birth and blood we also belong—a community of heritage and love which we enter by the new birth, saved by Jesus' blood. In this home we grow up in Christ, nourished in the ministry of God's word, strengthened by fellowship with our brothers and sisters, fortified by the sacraments, and enriched by the corporate worship which is offered there. So it was in the earliest days of Christianity, and so it is today. "And they continued steadfastly in the apostles' doctrine and fellowship, in the breaking of bread, and in prayers."[1]

> **The church is God's family.**

Jesus Himself established the church. "On this rock I will build My church; and the gates of hell shall not prevail against

---

[1] Acts 2:42.

it."[2] Here He speaks of the universal fellowship of the faithful, the great house of prayer for all nations, which He would build on the central truth which Peter had just confessed: "You are the Christ, the Son of the living God." But not only did He declare that He Himself would be the church's sure foundation, but also that He would guarantee its triumph. Against the most terrible opposition, it continues to confess His name, for He has promised, "The gates of hell shall not prevail!"

Very carefully Jesus gathered a little flock of followers who would do His work after He had returned to heaven. He chose, discipled, and ordained men who would become the church's missionaries and superintendents. Then not long before His death and resurrection, He established two sacred practices or sacraments which were to continue in His church until His return. First was baptism,[3] in which new Christians were to confess faith in Him publicly and enter the church fellowship; and second was the Lord's Supper,[4] which was to be a continuing reminder of His death for them.

Pentecost was the birthday of the New Testament church. Jesus' followers had assembled in Jerusalem, as He had commanded them, to wait for the promise of the Father. The Holy Spirit fell upon them, making visible the church that would be the body of Christ in the world, and launching the development of the church's structure. Peter preached the gospel to the assembled crowds, quoting from the Old Testament prophet Joel. Then they that gladly received his word were baptized: and the same day there were added to them about three thousand souls.[5]

In the New Testament, there were no church-less Christians. Those first believers loved the Church because they loved Jesus. For as the Scriptures teach, the Church "is His body, the fullness

---

2   Matthew 16:18.
3   **Matthew 28:19** "Go therefore and make disciples of all the nations, baptizing them in the name of the Father and of the Son and of the Holy Spirit."
4   **1 Corinthians 11:23-26** "For I received from the Lord that which I also delivered unto you . . . For as often as you eat this bread and drink this cup, you proclaim the Lord's death till He comes."
5   Acts 2:41.

of Him who fills all in all;"[6] and He is its living Head, "from whom the whole body [is] joined and knit together by what every joint supplies."[7]

As its living Head, Jesus is always present in the church by the Holy Spirit. As Jesus' body, the church is the group in fellowship which exists to do His will and to represent the interests of His Kingdom.[8] Never is the Head without the body, nor the body without the Head. Forever Christ is united to His church; and whoever is united to Christ is united to it, for we are members of His body, of His flesh, and of His bones.[9]

God has given supernatural abilities to members in the church, called spiritual gifts, so that members can serve one another.[10] These gifts do not signal levels of spiritual attainment, nor are they for personal profit. Because God distributes different spiritual gifts as He chooses,[11] no Christian is to assume personal credit for any spiritual gift that he has.

> **The church by nature draws in all kinds of sinners.**

Sometimes we are disappointed by professing Christians whose attitudes and actions are unworthy of Christ's name. We must remember that from the beginning the outward visible church has contained both those who are truly saved and those who only claim to be. This is proved by the story of Ananias and Sapphira.[12] At the same time, the invisible church consists only of those who are truly converted to Christ and who are joined to Him in living faith. As theologian Thomas Oden has pointed out, the presence of hypocrites and false members is because the

---

6 Ephesians 1:23.
7 Ephesians 4:16.
8 We are told to pray, "Your kingdom come, your will be done on earth as it is in heaven" (Matthew 6:10).
9 Ephesians 5:30.
10 1 Corinthians 12:12-26.
11 1 Corinthians 12:4-6, 11, 18, 4:7.
12 Acts 5:1-11.

church by nature draws in all kinds of sinners, with the intention of redeeming them.

Essential Characteristics of the Church

Through many centuries, Christians have understood the Bible to set down four essential characteristics of Christ's true church.

- ➡ The Church is one body. All believers constitute one body, for they have one head and are united with each other in Him. "There is one body, and one Spirit, just as you were called in one hope of your calling; one Lord, one faith, one baptism, one God and Father of all, who is above all, and through all, and in you all."[13]

Though there is one church, yet it is manifested in local bodies of believers, which can be called "churches."[14] Though there is one body, yet the local group of believers is called to function as the local body of Christ.[15]

- ➡ The Church is holy. Jesus, who separated the church from the world to represent Him in the world, has given Himself for it; "that He might sanctify and cleanse it with the washing of water by the word, that He might present it to Himself a glorious church, not having spot or wrinkle, or any such thing; but that it should be holy and without blemish."[16] The gospel which it preaches is holy, the discipline which it practices is holy, and all its true and living members are holy.

- ➡ The church is universal.[17] It is comprehensive in what it teaches and in the believers whom it includes, for it teaches all the truth necessary to our salvation and embraces all true believers, regardless of their cultural, racial, or denominational differences, and includes all the faithful, both in heaven and on earth.

---

13 Ephesians 4:4-6.
14 In Revelation chapters 2 & 3, letters are written to local "churches."
15 **Ephesians 4:4** "There is one body and one Spirit . . ."
16 Ephesians 5:25-27.
17 **Matthew 16:18** " . . . on this rock I will build my church, and the gates of Hades shall not prevail against it."

→ The church is apostolic. It preaches the true gospel which the apostles of our Lord received from Him and proclaimed as the faith once and for all delivered unto the saints.[18] The apostles committed it to faithful successors,[19] who passed it on to the following generations.

The Church's Functions—Our Responsibilities

Since the church is basic to God's purpose for us as Christians, its functions show us our responsibilities as its faithful members.

→ The church is a great temple of praise, "Offering up on every shore/ Her pure sacrifice of love," as an old hymn declares. You are the temple of the living God.[20] This means that we should join joyfully and enthusiastically in the public worship of the church.

→ The church is the witness and guardian of the gospel, for it is called "the pillar and ground of the truth."[21] Thus the church is God's instrument for upholding His word throughout the world; and as its members we must support its ministry by our money, our prayers, and our service.

→ The church is the teacher of the faithful, warning and teaching every man in all wisdom, that we may present every man perfect in Christ Jesus,[22] as did St. Paul, and teaching and admonishing one another in psalms and hymns and spiritual songs, singing with grace in your hearts to the Lord.[23] It is a Christian community where fellowship nurtures believers. We should carefully listen to the church's instruction and humbly obey its warnings.

---

18 **Jude 3** ". . . contend earnestly for the faith which was once for all delivered to the saints."
19 **2 Timothy 2:2** "And the things that you have heard from me among many witnesses, commit these to faithful men who will be able to teach others also."
20 2 Corinthians 6:16.
21 1 Timothy 3:15.
22 Colossians 1:28.
23 Colossians 3:16.

→ The church is an agent for moral reform, bringing renewal and spiritual enlightenment to the entire world. You are the salt of the earth ... you are the light of the world ... So let your light so shine before men, that they may see your good works, and glorify your Father in heaven.[24] Behind this effort and witness we are called upon to throw our full support.

→ The church is a great evangelistic agency to take the Gospel everywhere. "Go therefore and make disciples of all the nations, baptizing them in the name of the Father and of the Son and of the Holy Spirit, teaching them to observe all things that I have commanded you; and lo, I am with you always, even unto the end of the age."[25] Each of us is a full partner in this great cause, for the Great Commission is for us all.

Yes, home is where the heart is. In all of us is a deep desire for home and family, where by birth and blood we belong. Our spiritual home is the church—a community with a deep heritage and love which we enter by the new birth, saved by the blood of Jesus. Christianity is about personal relationship with Him, but it is also about community relationship with His people. We belong to Him and we belong to one another. We belong at home!

I Believe . . .
The church is established by Jesus to be one, worldwide, holy, and faithful to the apostles' doctrine. The church is to be a congregation of praise, a witness to the truth, a community for discipleship, an influence for reformation, and a force for proclamation of the gospel. The church is where I am at home, because God is my Father and His people are my family.

---

[24] Matthew 5:13, 14, 16.
[25] Matthew 28:19-20.

Questions for Study

1. In what sense is church the home of the believer?
2. What promise did Jesus make about the ultimate triumph of the church?
3. What two sacraments did Jesus institute, and what does each mean?
4. What is the purpose of spiritual gifts?
5. Why should we not be surprised to see sinners in the church?
6. What are four distinguishing characteristics of the church?
7. What are five purposes of the church?

Recommended Reading

Noll, Mark. *Turning Points*. Grand Rapids, MI: Baker Academic, 1997.

Oden, Thomas. *Life in the Spirit*. Peabody, MA: Prince Press, 2001.

16

Christ's Triumphant Return

"**J**esus is coming soon!" Those words once filled me with fear and confusion. If I doubted that I was prepared, I feared being "left behind!" If I was "ready," I was filled with disappointment that my plans for life would never be realized. Indeed the "Second Coming of Christ" evokes emotions of confusion, excitement, fear, and hope. What will this event be like? How will it impact us?

What does it mean that Christ is coming again?

Jesus will return visibly to this earth. Though He is spiritually present with believers on the earth now,[1] He will at that time appear in His glorified, risen form in the sight of all the earth.[2]

What will happen at the return of Christ?

The return of Christ will be the climax of earthly history. The kingdoms of the world will become the kingdoms of Christ. Those who have been faithful to Him will be rewarded and honored. Those who have been in rebellion against Him will be put down, and He will have power that will overcome all opposition.[3] Every knee will bow, and every tongue will confess that Jesus is Lord.[4]

---

1 **Matthew 28:20** " . . . lo, I am with you always, even to the end of the age. Amen."
2 **Revelation 1:7** "Behold, He is coming with clouds, and every eye will see Him, and they also who pierced Him. And all the tribes of the earth will mourn because of Him. Even so, Amen."
3 **Matthew 26:64** "Jesus said to him, 'It is as you said. Nevertheless, I say to you, hereafter you will see the Son of Man sitting at the right hand of the Power, and coming on the clouds of heaven.'"
4 **Philippians 2:10** "That at the name of Jesus every knee should bow, of those in heaven, and of those on earth, and of those under the earth."

Christians of the past will be resurrected to rule with Christ.[5] They and the living believers will rise to meet the Lord when He appears.[6] The devil will be chained so that he will tempt and deceive no longer.[7]

How do we know that Jesus is coming again?

The Old Testament anticipates the Second Coming. We are told that One will come "like a son of man," "on the clouds of heaven."[8] Jesus told us that He would return with power and glory.[9] He promised to come and take His people to live with Him.[10] The angels declared it at the time of Jesus' ascension. They said that He would return in the same manner that He had ascended into Heaven.[11] The apostles proclaimed it. They saw the time before Christ's return as a time to preach repentance while waiting for Christ to return to establish God's ultimate plan for this world.[12] Throughout the New Testament the Second Coming is prophesied.[13] That Jesus will return to this earth again in power and glory is one of the most widely taught truths in the New Testament.

---

5 **2 Timothy 2:12** "If we endure, we shall also reign with Him. If we deny Him, He will also deny us."
6 **1 Thessalonians 4:16-17** "For the Lord Himself will descend from heaven with a shout, with the voice of an archangel, and with the trumpet of God. And the dead in Christ will rise first. Then we who are alive and remain shall be caught up together with them in the clouds to meet the Lord in the air. And thus shall we ever be with the Lord."
7 **Revelation 20:2-3** "He laid hold of the dragon, that serpent of old, who is the devil and Satan, and bound him for a thousand years; and he cast him into the bottomless pit, and shut him up, and set a seal on him, so that he should deceive the nations no more . . ."
8 Daniel 7:13-14.
9 **Matthew 24:30** "Then the sign of the Son of Man will appear in heaven, and then all the tribes of the earth will mourn, and they will see the Son of Man coming on the clouds of heaven with power and great glory."
10 **John 14:3** "And if I go and prepare a place for you, I will come again and receive you to Myself; that where I am, there you may be also."
11 **Acts 1:11** "This same Jesus, who was taken up from you into heaven, will so come in like manner as you saw Him go into heaven."
12 **Acts 3:19-21** "Repent therefore and be converted that your sins may be blotted out . . . and that He may send Jesus Christ who was preached to you before, whom heaven must receive until the times of restoration of all things . . ."
13 I Thessalonians 4:15-16; II Thessalonians 1:7, 10; Titus 2:13; Hebrews 9:28; James 5:7-8; I Peter 1:7, 13; II Peter 1:16; 3:4, 12; I John 2:28.

When will He come again?

Though there are signs that will precede the Second Coming, we cannot know exactly when He will return. It is good for believers to always anticipate Jesus' coming and to live accordingly.[14]

There have been great debates over whether Jesus would come back before certain other events and periods that the Bible predicts, such as the coming of the antichrist and the tribulation period. Even among conservative evangelical believers, there has been much disagreement over these questions.

In spite of these questions, we must remember the priorities that early Christians had. The main concern is not whether or not we will escape certain hard times; after all, the church in various places has suffered hard times for centuries, and we are called to keep our faith and "endure to the end." We are warned not to let materialism make us forget about the coming. We are told to "watch," not gazing at the sky for His appearance, but staying on guard spiritually so that His coming will not catch us unprepared.[15] Those who live today as though He is not coming probably will not be ready for His return, whenever it is.[16]

For most people, life will be going on normally when Jesus returns.[17] This reality ought to challenge every believer to make sure that his "normal" life is to live faithfully to God. Jesus' coming will be like lightning or the twinkling of an eye,[18] so sudden that nobody will have time to make any changes after He appears.

---

14 **Mark 13:33-37** "Take heed, watch and pray; for you do not know when the time is . . . lest, coming suddenly, he find you sleeping. And what I say to you, I say to all: Watch!"
15 The term used for "watch" does not refer to looking for something but to staying on guard.
16 1 Thessalonians 5:1-6 shows that those who are in darkness, living for this world, will be the ones shocked by the return of the Lord. For us, He will not return "as a thief."
17 Matthew 24:36-44 describes people partying, having celebrations, and going about routine tasks when the time of judgment comes.
18 Matthew 24:27, 1 Corinthians 15:52.

Why has He waited so long?

Throughout history believers have anticipated Jesus' return to be very near. Modern skeptics ridicule this faith because of the long delay of Jesus' return.[19] However, while realizing that Jesus' return has not been as soon as many believers expected, we should note the following:

- ➡ Only God knows the time of Jesus' return.[20] The time for Jesus' return will not be impulsive; it is perfectly planned.[21] Just as Jesus was born to save the world at the *best* time,[22] Jesus' Second Coming will be at the *best* time.

- ➡ Parables teach that Jesus' Second Coming will follow a period of time that is long enough for people to become careless concerning His return.[23]

- ➡ We live by the clock and the calendar and cannot understand God's concept of time from the perspective of eternity.[24]

- ➡ The time of the return has been prolonged in order to grant more people the opportunity to be saved. He delays because He desires that none should perish.[25]

Why will He come?

We live in a world where humanity, though created in the image of God, is mostly in rebellion against God. The whole creation suffers from the curse of sin. This is not a condition that God

---

19 **2 Peter 3:3-4** "Knowing this first: that scoffers will come in the last days, walking according to their own lusts, and saying, 'Where is the promise of His coming? For since the fathers fell asleep, all things continue as they were from the beginning of creation.'"
20 **Matthew 24:36** "But of that day and hour no one knows, no, not even the angels of heaven, but My Father only."
21 **Acts 1:7** "And He said to them, 'It is not for you to know times or seasons which the Father has put in His own authority.'"
22 **Galatians 4:4** "But when the fullness of the time had come, God sent forth His Son, born of a woman, born under the law.'"
23 See Matthew 24:45-51, 25:5, 19, Luke 19:11-27.
24 **2 Peter 3:8** "But, beloved, do not forget this one thing, that with the Lord one day is as a thousand years, and a thousand years as one day."
25 **2 Peter 3:9** "The Lord is not slack concerning His promise, as some count slackness, but is longsuffering toward us, not willing that any should perish but that all should come to repentance."

will tolerate forever, but what is His solution? The world will never be made better by political action, social reform, improved education, or prosperous economies. Neither will the world's improvement occur gradually. Jesus will suddenly enter His creation as the returning king, to set it right. Satan is already judged, and those who follow Satan in his rebellion will also be condemned.

> Jesus will suddenly enter His creation as the returning king.

All people are sinners, but God is now offering them a chance to receive forgiveness. If they willingly join His kingdom now, they can escape the coming judgment on all rebels. God's kingdom is being planted in the hearts of those who repent and believe, even in a world that is in rebellion. That kingdom will come fully and openly at the return of Jesus.

Then how should we live?

Those who live in expectation of His coming seek the purity that His grace makes possible. They live in spiritual victory over sin.[26] They stay on guard spiritually by prayer.[27]

They live according to eternal values, since the things of this world will pass away. They are willing, if necessary, to give up even the good things of this life, knowing that the One who created earthly blessings has planned even more wonderful things for eternity. It would be a foolish mistake for one to give up eternity for the sake of what he can have now, as if he thinks that God's imagination has been spent, and there can be nothing better than what he can see.

If we live in expectation of His coming, we will be conscious of the mission He has given us. We will not focus on establishing a personal utopia here, like a person laying carpet in the cabin of a sink-

---

26 **1 John 3:3** "And everyone who has this hope in Him purifies himself, just as He is pure."
27 **Mark 13:33** "Take heed, watch and pray; for you do not know what the time is."

ing ship, or straightening pictures on the wall of a burning house. We must focus on saving the people around us who are perishing.

> **I Believe . . .**
> Jesus will return as He promised, resurrecting believers of the past, and taking all believers to reign in His kingdom. Evil powers will be defeated. As believers, we must spread the gospel and live by eternal values, ready for the Lord's return.

Questions for Study

1. Who will see Jesus when He returns?
2. What will happen to evil powers at that time?
3. What will happen to Christians at that time?
4. What about Christians who die before the coming of the Lord?
5. What does it mean to "watch" and be ready?
6. How does the Bible describe the suddenness of Jesus' coming?
7. Why has it been so long until the coming of the Lord?
8. Will the world be changed gradually or suddenly?
9. How should we live because of expecting the Lord's return? (3 parts)

Recommended Reading

Ladd, George Eldon. *The Blessed Hope*. Grand Rapids, MI: Eerdmans, 1992.

Wiley, H. Orton & Culbertson, Paul T. *Introduction to Christian Theology*. Kansas City, MO: Beacon Hill Press, 1949.

17

Heaven—Eternal Life with God

Let not your heart be troubled: ye believe in God, believe also in me. In my Father's house are many mansions: if it were not so, I would have told you. I go to prepare a place for you. And if I go and prepare a place for you I will come again, and receive you unto myself, that where I am, there ye may be also.[1]

Jesus' words tell us some things about heaven. Most important is that heaven is God's home. Another fact that is important to us is that we can someday live there with God.

The promise of heaven should guide the way we live on earth. People used to say critically that someone was "Too heavenly minded to be of any earthly good," but the person who lives by eternal values will do the most good on earth. The person who expects a heavenly reward has an incentive to endure hardship of all kinds and strive to accomplish God's will. Jesus says to the one in persecution, "Rejoice, for great is your reward in heaven."[2]

There are many things we cannot understand about heaven. Because we are flesh and blood, we can't comprehend the nature of God's existence, for He is Spirit. Besides, God's nature is infinite, beyond our understanding, so we cannot fully understand what His home is like.

We know only what God has revealed to us about this place. In Scripture He has given us glimpses of some aspects that we

---

[1] John 14:1-3.
[2] Matthew 5:12.

can partially comprehend, but the realities of Heaven transcend even these glimpses.

All of creation exists for the glory of God, but heaven is the central scene of the universe, where God is worshipped at the highest level by the creatures He made in His image. Look at the scene of worship described in Revelation 5:11-14.

God's glory will be revealed in heaven in such fullness that it will be the light of the city.[3] It is the place where we will so know God that we will "see His face."[4]

Worship is the business of heaven. Joy is the other side of worship. A psalm writer said, "In Your presence is fullness of joy; at Your right hand are pleasures forevermore."[5] An old Presbyterian catechism says that the "chief end of man" is "to worship God and enjoy Him forever." It is fitting that joy and worship are so connected. God created us in His image, so that we could understand His nature enough to worship Him for who He is. Our emotions, ability to love, and intelligence are all given so that we can give God the highest possible worship.

> **It is fitting that joy and worship are so connected.**

Characteristics of Heaven

Sometimes people on earth cannot buy the home they want, and they may not be able to make their home into all that they want it to be. But God has infinite power and resources, so we know that His home is exactly what He wants it to be. Therefore, heaven is perfectly consistent with the nature of God.

---

3   **Revelation 21:23** "And the city had no need of the sun or of the moon to shine in it, for the glory of God illuminated it, and the Lamb is its light."
4   Revelation 22:4, also 1 John 3:2.
5   Psalm 16:11.

We know about some of the characteristics of heaven because of details revealed in Scripture and because God has revealed His own nature to us.

There will be no sin in heaven. All the beings in heaven, whether angels or redeemed earthlings, will be completely holy.[6]

Heaven will be free from all of the results of sin, including pain, sorrow, conflicts, and danger.[7] There will be no more of the curse upon creation, including sickness, aging, and death.[8]

The beauty of heaven is beyond description. Details given to us include walls of jasper, gates of pearl, foundations of rare gems, and streets of gold.[9]

Heaven is populated by millions of angels and redeemed people.[10]

Some Questions about Heaven

➡ **Where is Heaven?**

We do not know where Heaven is. The Bible speaks of Heaven as being up, and of God's looking down from Heaven. Simply put, Heaven is not here on this earth.

➡ **Who goes to Heaven?**

Heaven is prepared for those who have repented of sin and believe in (entrust their lives to) Jesus Christ as Savior and Lord.[11]

---

6   **Revelation 21:8** "But the cowardly, unbelieving, abominable, murderers, sexually immoral, sorcerers, idolaters, and all liars shall have their part in the lake which burns with fire and brimstone, which is the second death."
7   **Revelation 21:4** "And God will wipe away every tear from their eyes; there shall be no more death, nor sorrow, nor crying; and there shall be no more pain, for the former things have passed away."
8   **Revelation 22:3** "And there shall be no more curse, but the throne of God and of the Lamb shall be in it, and His servants shall serve Him."
9   This description comes from details given of the New Jerusalem (Revelation 21:18-21).
10   **Revelation 5:8-11** "Then I looked, and I heard the voice of many angels around the throne, the living creatures, and the elders [representing redeemed people, see the previous two verses] and the number of them was ten thousand times ten thousand, and thousands of thousands."
11   **John 3:16** "For God so loved the world that He gave His only begotten Son, that whoever believes in Him should not perish but have everlasting life."

Those whose names are written in Heaven[12] will inhabit Heaven. We can live for (invest in and value) Heaven, and those who value the things that Heaven values will store there that which lasts forever.[13]

➡ When does one go to Heaven?

Jesus told the thief dying on the cross that they would be together in paradise that day.[14] Paul said that to be absent from the body is to be present with the Lord.[15] Therefore, we know that the believer goes to heaven at the time of death. However, believers who are still alive at the return of Jesus will go to heaven without passing through death.[16]

➡ What if I feel disappointed about someday leaving behind the good parts of earthly life?

Many young people hope that they will not go to heaven before enjoying marriage. A person in a happy marriage may dread the day when that marriage will be ended by death, even if he expects to go to heaven. There are many other aspects of earthly life that are good because they are designed by God, and we may wish they would never end. The thing to remember is that God is the One who created all those things for this earthly life. Surely He is able to exceed all of that for the eternal life in heaven! We can have faith that heaven will exceed our expectations, satisfy us completely, and not be a disappointment in any way.

---

12 **Luke 10:20** "Nevertheless do not rejoice in this, that the spirits are subject to you, but rather rejoice because your names are written in heaven."

  Revelation 3:5 "He who overcomes shall be clothed in white garments, and I will not blot out his name from the Book of Life; but I will confess his name before My Father and before His angels."

13 **Matthew 6:20** "But lay up for yourselves treasures in heaven, where neither moth nor rust destroys and where thieves do not break in and steal."

14 **Luke 23:43** "And Jesus said to him, 'Assuredly, I say to you, today you will be with Me in Paradise.'"

15 **2 Corinthians 5:8** "We are confident, yes, well pleased rather to be absent from the body and to be present with the Lord."

16 **1 Corinthians 15:51-52** "Behold, I tell you a mystery: We shall not all sleep, but we shall all be changed—in a moment, in the twinkling of an eye, at the last trumpet. For the trumpet will sound, and the dead will be raised incorruptible, and we shall be changed."

Think of the words of C.S. Lewis when you think of the cry of the human heart for the heavenly:

If I find in myself a desire which no experience in this world can satisfy, the most probable explanation is that I was made for another world. If none of my earthly pleasures satisfy it, that does not prove that the universe is a fraud. Probably earthly pleasures were never meant to satisfy it, but only to arouse it, to suggest the real thing. . . I must keep alive in myself the desire for my true country, which I shall not find till after death. . . I must make it the main object of life to press on to that other country and to help others do the same.[17]

I Believe . . .
Heaven is God's home, where I can live with God for eternity, joyfully worshipping Him. In heaven is no sin, nor any of the suffering that results from it. Heaven exceeds my imagination and will satisfy my heart. I will go to heaven either when I die or when Jesus returns.

Questions for Study

1. Why can we not fully understand heaven now?
2. Why does the nature of God tell us something about heaven?
3. What are some things that will not be in heaven?
4. What are some details given about heaven that show its beauty?
5. Who will go to heaven?
6. When will we go to heaven?
7. What if we feel disappointed when we think about leaving the good things of earth?

---

17   C.S. Lewis, *Mere Christianity*. HarperCollins.

Recommended Reading

Lewis, C. S. "The Weight of Glory," in *The Weight of Glory and Other Addresses*. New York: Macmillan Publishing, 1980.

Purkiser, W.T. *Exploring our Christian Faith*. Kansas City, MO: Beacon Hill, 1960.

18

Eternal Punishment

"If you choose in time to live without God, you thereby choose eternally to be without God" Hippolytus.

Anything said to be eternal should catch our attention, especially if it is punishment. Punishments on earth always end sometime. Whether they are whippings, suspensions, imprisonments, or banishments, the end comes, even if it is at the death of the one being punished.

But Jesus described a punishment that is everlasting when He said, "Depart from Me, you cursed, into the everlasting fire prepared for the devil and his angels...And these will go away into everlasting punishment, but the righteous into eternal life."[1]

> **Jesus mentioned hell more than heaven.**

Maybe this is one doctrine that we could wish were not taught in Scripture, but it is there. Jesus and the apostles affirmed that hell, the lake of fire, and eternal punishment exist. In fact, Jesus mentioned hell more than heaven. He often issued warnings for us to avoid this horrible place. Note a sampling of words on the subject from Jesus and the apostles.

"If your right eye causes you to sin, pluck it out and cast it from you; for it is more profitable for you that one of your members perish, than for your whole body to be cast into hell. And if your right hand causes you to sin,

---

1 Matthew 25:41, 46.

cut it off and cast it from you; for it is more profitable for you that one of your members perish, than for your whole body to be cast into hell."[2]

"So it will be at the end of the age. The angels will come forth, separate the wicked from among the just, and cast them into the furnace of fire. There will be wailing and gnashing of teeth."[3]

Speaking to the Pharisees, Jesus said, *"Serpents, brood of vipers! How can you escape the condemnation of hell?"*[4]

"And being in torment in Hades, he lifted up his eyes and saw Abraham afar off, and Lazarus in his bosom. Then he cried and said, 'Father Abraham, have mercy on me, and send Lazarus, that he may dip the tip of his finger in water, and cool my tongue; for I am tormented in this flame.'"[5]

The Apostle Paul writes that Jesus will be *"revealed from heaven with His mighty angels, in flaming fire taking vengeance on those who do not know God, and on those who do not obey the gospel of our Lord Jesus Christ. These shall be punished with everlasting destruction from the presence of the Lord and from the glory of His power."*[6]

"For if God did not spare the angels who sinned, but cast them down to hell and delivered them into chains of darkness, to be reserved for judgment."[7]

"The devil, who deceived them, was cast into the lake of fire and brimstone where the beast and the false prophet are. And they will be tormented day and night forever and ever...anyone not found written in the book of life was cast into the lake of fire."[8]

Notice the kind of words used to describe this place: fire, torment, vengeance, destruction, darkness, chains, judgment, crying, wailing, and gnashing of teeth. You would not expect any intelligent person to choose such a destiny for himself.

Jesus said that it would be better to gouge out your right eye and cut off your right hand than to be cast into hell with both eye and hand. Of course we are not headed for hell because of having a right eye and right hand, but if these lead us to commit sin, then

---

[2] Matthew 5:29-30.
[3] Matthew 13:49-50.
[4] Matthew 23:33.
[5] Luke 16:23-24.
[6] 1 Thessalonians 1:7-9.
[7] 2 Peter 2:4.
[8] Revelation 20:10, 15.

it would be better to be without them than to be cast into hell. Jesus was not encouraging the mutilation of the body, but the cutting off of any activity that would lead us to sin and consequently to hell, even if it seemed as important to us as our right eye and right hand.

The Bible tells us that death ends man's probation, and that hell is eternal, irrevocable, and agonizing. This biblical truth is rejected by atheists, who say there is nothing after death, and by Jehovah's Witnesses, Mormons, and Universalists, who say there is no hell. The fact that death ends man's probation is denied by Roman Catholics, who believe that the condition of some people will be remedied after death.

> **Death ends man's probation, and hell is eternal, irrevocable, and agonizing.**

There are those who deny the existence of hell because they consider it unjust. They say that if sin took place in a finite space of time, it could not be just for the punishment to be eternal. St. Augustine used to reply to this objection with the example of criminal law. If a robbery takes place in a few minutes, should one only have a few minutes' punishment? A rape that takes minutes may have consequences for a lifetime. A murder that takes only an instant is an irreparable damage. In Scripture, we discover that sin against an eternal and infinite God results in eternal punishment, even though it was committed in a finite lifetime.

Hell is eternal because sin is an offense against an infinite God. It is eternal because the sinner denies God the eternal worship and service owed. It is eternal because we are eternal beings with no other place to go if we choose separation from God.

We tend to recoil from the idea of a choice with eternal consequences. Children will often declare, "I quit," when a game is not going to their liking, but they want to have the option of reentering the game later. We like to think that there will be a second chance in the future, even if we are making a deliberate choice now. But is it unreasonable that God would limit our trial period to a lifetime?

Some refuse to believe in hell because they wonder how a loving God could send someone to such an awful place as these verses describe. We must keep in mind that God desires no one to be lost, but that all should come to repentance and salvation. The Bible states this emphatically in a number of places.[9] Those who go to hell have made choices that place them in this horrific place. No one accidentally stumbles into hell. Those who go have chosen the place by rejecting God, righteousness, and salvation. Since all that is good comes from God, rejection of God is eventually a rejection of all that is good. Surely we could not expect God to eternally supply a person with good things when that person has rejected God. Then hell, or separation from God, is all that is left.

> Is it unreasonable that God would limit our trial period to a lifetime?

Perhaps, instead of complaining, we ought to thank God that He will quarantine sin someday. What redeemed and righteous person would want to spend an eternity with an unredeemed and unrepentant murderer, rapist, liar, adulterer, or thief? As it is a father's love that protects his children against a harmful intruder, so it is God's love that brings justice to those who would harm and destroy their fellow man.

In spite of current objections to hell, we believe that Scripture teaches that such a place exists, that it is a place of agonizing punishment for the unrepentant wicked, that it lasts forever, and that the love of God is not compromised by its existence.

Let me briefly paraphrase C.S. Lewis:

---

[9] I Timothy 2:4, II Peter 2:9, Acts 17:30.

"Ultimately the objections to the doctrine of hell must come to this question: "What are you asking God to do?" To wipe out their past sins and give a fresh start, assisting in difficulty with miraculous help? But He has offered to do so. To forgive them? But they refuse to be forgiven. To leave them alone? Alas, I am afraid that is what He does."[10]

Thank God that through the atoning work of Jesus Christ, His love has made it possible for us to "escape the wrath to come." Instead of the agonies of hell, we may share in the grandeur of salvation and heaven, and this becomes possible when we exercise "repentance toward God and faith in our Lord Jesus Christ."[11]

I Believe . . .
Hell is the eternal, irrevocable, and agonizing place of punishment for all who have not been saved from their sins by Christ. Hell is the just punishment for willful sin against an infinite God.

Questions for Study

1. What did Jesus mean when He said that it would be better to cut off your hand than to go to hell?

2. What are three words that best summarize hell?

3. What are some groups of people who deny the existence of hell?

4. Why is hell eternal?

5. How can we escape being condemned to hell?

Discussion question: How would you answer someone who says that hell is unjust and contrary to the love of God?

---

10 Lewis, *The Problem of Pain*, 128.
11 Acts 20:21.

Recommended Reading

Purkiser, W.T. *Exploring Our Christian Faith*. Kansas City, MO: Beacon Hill Press, 1967. Especially chapter xxviii, "The Future Life."

Wesley, John. "The Great Assize," in Wesley's *52 Standard Sermons*. Salem, OH: Schmul Publishing, 1988.

19

Final Events

The mark of the beast, the seals and the trumpets, the great tribulation, the antichrist, the sounding of the trumpet, the 1,000 years, the 7 years, the great white throne, the city descending, the lake of fire—what do you think of when biblical prophecy is mentioned?

Levels of Importance

Unfortunately, debates over interpretation of prophecy often focus on minor questions instead of the major truths. Topics in prophecy should be divided into levels of importance.

➡ The lowest level of importance could be called "speculative issues." Some examples of speculative issues could be wondering what the mark of the beast will look like, what country the antichrist will come from, and who the two witnesses will be. These are questions that the Bible does not clearly answer, and disputing over them is hardly worth the time.

➡ The next level of importance could be called "controversies among evangelicals." These are topics that the Bible does explain, and it is not inappropriate for a person to have a firm opinion on them. However, even intelligent people who believe the Bible have never been in complete agreement on these questions. Therefore, you should never break fellowship with someone because he seems to have the wrong position on one of these controversies. Some examples would be whether Jesus will come back at the beginning, middle, or end of the tribulation; and whether or not the millennium is a literal thousand years.

- ➡ The highest level of importance contains "necessary truths." These are truths that are so clear and emphasized in the Bible that a person could scarcely claim to believe the Bible while denying them. To deny them also has immediate effects on practical living.

Let's look at four necessary truths revealed in biblical prophecy about final events.

The Physical Return of Jesus

A tour guide in an old Friend's church in Philadelphia said, "We don't have any doctrine; doctrine divides." When asked what her church believed about how a person could get to heaven, she said, "I think some people put too much focus on heaven; if they would forget about heaven, they might do more good making the world a better place."

> The return of Jesus will be the great climax of all that God is doing in the world.

This is a typical expression of what has been called the "social gospel." Rather than seeing Christianity as a message emphasizing the spiritual and eternal, some want to emphasize only the good that Christianity can do on earth. The focus is on what man can do rather than on what God can do and will do. Most of those who deny that Jesus will come back have oriented themselves to earthly life and are concentrating on making their conditions here the best they can.

Just as the cross of Christ marks the pivot point of all history, the return of Jesus will be the great climax of all that God is doing in the world. His return is the inevitable conclusion of the age when the message of the cross has been proclaimed. Those who have accepted it will be accepted by God.[1] Those who have rejected and persecuted His truth will experience His wrath.[2]

Our expectation of His return is the blessed hope of all Christians.[3] In fact, most of the occurrences of the word *hope* in the New Testament refer to aspects of salvation that will be fulfilled at the coming of the Lord.

> **The return of Jesus will be the great climax of all that God is doing in the world.**

Think of all that His return means to us: the end of persecution, suffering, and sorrow; reunion with saints and Christian loved ones; proof that our faith has not been in vain, as faith becomes sight; the sight of Jesus Himself; and entrance into heaven and the fullness of eternal life with God. None of these things depend on the time of His return, but simply on the fact that He will return as He promised. We are told to expect Him and to endure in faith. The fact that He will return is an essential Christian doctrine.

The Bodily Resurrection of All People

It has been said that if the human body were valued according to the minerals it contains, it would be worth only a few dollars. Of course, we know that such an approach to evaluating the body is ridiculous, because the body is valued for its life, its usefulness, and other considerations much more important than the minerals it contains.

Does the body have eternal value? Some Christians seem to think not. They seem to think that a person is actually the soul, and

---

[1] **2 Thessalonians 1:7** "And to give you who are troubled rest with us when the Lord Jesus is revealed from heaven with His mighty angels, in flaming fire taking vengeance on those who do not know God, and on those who do not obey the gospel of our Lord Jesus Christ."
[2] **Revelation 6:16-17** "Fall on us and hide us from the face of Him who sits on the throne and from the wrath of the Lamb! For the great day of His wrath has come, and who shall be able to stand."
[3] **Titus 2:13** "Looking for the blessed hope and glorious appearing of our great God and Savior Jesus Christ."

the body only its home. They speak as though the body will be discarded forever when someone dies. That is not the true Christian view, for the Bible teaches the resurrection of all people.

> **The belief that we will someday be resurrected affects our lifestyle.**

What would happen if we were persuaded that we will not be physically raised from the dead? The Apostle Paul explained in 1 Corinthians 15 that to deny the resurrection would be to deny the gospel. If there is no resurrection, then Jesus could not have been raised.[4] If Jesus did not rise from the dead, the gospel cannot be true, and nobody is really saved.[5]

Every person will be resurrected, but not all people at the same time. At the return of Jesus, He will take up all Christians, resurrecting those who have died.[6]

> "Blessed and holy is he who has part in the first resurrection. Over such the second death has no power, but they shall be priests of God and of Christ, and shall reign with Him a thousand years."[7]

Those who are not accepted for the first resurrection are those who die in their sins. They are raised at a later time to stand judgment.

> "The sea gave up the dead who were in it, and Death and Hades delivered up the dead who were in them, And they were judged, each one according to his works . . . And anyone not found in the Book of Life was cast into the lake of fire."[8]

---

4   **1 Corinthians 15:13** "But if there is no resurrection of the dead, then Christ is not risen."
5   **1 Corinthians 15:17** "And if Christ is not risen, your faith is futile; you are still in your sins!"
6   **1 Thessalonians 4:16-17** "For the Lord Himself will descend from heaven with a shout, with the voice of an archangel, and with the trumpet of God. And the dead in Christ will rise first. Then we who are alive and remain shall be caught up together with them in the clouds to meet the Lord in the air, And thus we shall always be with the Lord."
7   Revelation 20:6.
8   Revelation 20:13.

More than we realize, the belief that we will someday be resurrected affects our lifestyle. We can see the practical effects of the doctrine by looking at the examples of people who deny it. Some people in the Corinthian church were denying that the human body will be resurrected.[9] Those who believed this error divided into two extreme positions. Some seemed to say, "Since the body will not be raised, the spirit is all that matters. That means that the sins we commit with the body are not serious. We can even commit fornication, because the body is going to be discarded anyway."[10]

Others said something like, "Since the body will not be raised, it must be worthless and evil. We should suppress all bodily desires, not eating anything that tastes pleasant or enjoying marriage."[11]

Both of these errors came from denying the resurrection. The Christian doctrine of the resurrection puts value on the body. Value is shown in that the Christians' bodies are redeemed, are temples of the Holy Spirit, are members of Christ, and will be resurrected and glorified.[12]

"You were bought with a price; therefore glorify God in your body and in your spirit, which are God's."

---

[9] This is shown by the fact that Paul wrote a passage of 58 verses (all of 1 Corinthians 15) defending the doctrine of the resurrection.

[10] See 1 Corinthians 6:13-14, where some seemed to have a slogan, "Foods for the stomach and the stomach for foods," meaning that the body is for nothing but indulgence of desires. The apostle said, "But God will destroy both it and them," speaking of judgment for the misuse of the body. He goes on to say, "The body is for the Lord . . . And God both raised up the Lord and will also raise us up by His power."

[11] See 1 Corinthians 7:1-2, where Paul spoke to some who were suggesting that Christians should not have any sexual relationship, including marriage. This was an extreme opposite to the one discussed in the verses right before, but also probably came from doubting the resurrection, and therefore devaluing the body.

[12] **1 Corinthians 6:14, 15, 19, 20** "And God . . . will also raise us up by His power. . . Do you not know that your bodies are members of Christ? . . Or do you not know that your body is the temple of the Holy Spirit? . . For you were bought with a price; therefore glorify God in your body and in your spirit which are God's."

The Judgment of All People

> *Then I saw a great white throne and Him who sat upon it, from whose face the earth and the heaven fled away. And there was found no place for them. And I saw the dead, small and great, standing before God, and books were opened. And another book was opened, which is the Book of Life. And the dead were judged according to their works, by the things which were written in the books. The sea gave up the dead who were in it, and Death and Hades delivered up the dead who were in them. And they were judged, each one according to his works. Then Death and Hades were cast into the lake of fire. This is the second death. And anyone not found written in the Book of Life was cast into the lake of fire.*[13]

We cannot help but feel the sense of finality emphasized in this scene. This is truly the end for those whose names are not in the Book of Life. It is not the end of their existence, but it is the end of their making of choices. The eternity that follows will be unending consequences of decisions that can never be reversed.

Those who deny a final judgment seek to lower the significance of human choices. They want to feel that anything we do wrong today may be corrected someday. But the Bible says that "now is the day of salvation."[14] There will come a time when decision making is over and only consequences will remain.

The fact of the coming judgment gives our choices significance beyond their immediate results. That is something sinners want to deny. They want to think that as long as they can control the immediate results of their actions, there is nothing else to worry about. One counselor on talk radio said to a caller, "I think that there is nothing wrong except irresponsible behavior." She explained that in her opinion, if you can take responsibility for the results of what you are doing, there is nothing else to worry about. But God's word says that people will be judged for their works.[15]

---

[13] Revelation 20:11-15.
[14] 2 Corinthians 6:2.
[15] **2 Corinthians 5:10** "For we must all appear before the judgment seat of Christ, that each one may receive the things done in the body, according to what he has done, whether good or bad."

Judgment will conclude with the sentencing of some to eternal punishment and the granting of eternal reward to others.[16] Not everyone will necessarily be judged at the same time. Scripture describes one scene of judgment that seems to be for sinners who are resurrected in order to face condemnation for their sinful works.[17] There is another judgment for Christians, where they will be rewarded for those works that had worthwhile, lasting results.[18]

God does not intend that we live in constant fear, and that fear be our motive for living right. However, consciousness of the judgment ahead gives us a sense of accountability that guides our lives.

> **There will come a time when decision making is over and only consequences will remain.**

> [God] 'will render to each one according to his deeds:' eternal life to those who by patient continuance in doing good seek for glory, honor, and immortality; but to those who are self-seeking and do not obey the truth, but obey unrighteousness—indignation and wrath, tribulation and anguish, on every soul of man who does evil, of the Jew first and also of the Greek; but glory, honor, and peace to everyone who works what is good, to the Jew first and also to the Greek. For there is no partiality with God.[19]

God's Eternal Kingdom

According to the Bible, time has a beginning and a clear series of events progressing to a conclusion. The Bible begins with creation, depicts the tragic fall of man, then records God's working

---

16 For further scriptural description of eternal punishment, see the chapter in this book on that topic.
17 See Revelation 20:11-15, partially quoted earlier in this chapter. There do not seem to be any Christians being judged in this scene, because they were previously resurrected and rewarded (see verses 4-6).
18 **1 Corinthians 3:14-15** "If anyone's work which he has built on it endures [the test described in the previous verse], he will receive a reward. If anyone's work is burned, he will suffer loss; but he himself will be saved, yet so as through fire."
19 Romans 2:6-11.

out the plan of salvation amidst centuries of human history. Life as we know it has not always been and will not always be.

In Genesis we find the beginning of sin. In Revelation sin is absolutely excluded from God's eternal city.[20] In Genesis we see the loss of the tree of life and the sentence of death. In Revelation we see restoration of the tree of life, names in the Book of Life, and invitation to a river of the water of life.[21]

In this chapter we have mentioned many future events, discussed a few of them, and only referred to the debates about timing. But we know that there is one event that will come at the end of the schedule as God has revealed it to us. This event will launch the universe into the eternity that God has planned. It will be the coming of God's complete and eternal kingdom.

As Creator, God has always been the King of His universe, but since the fall of man, humanity has mostly been in rebellion against God's kingdom. That is going to come to a sudden end, and God will rule eternally without a rival.

This poetic and graphic scene is from the book of Daniel.[22]

> I watched till thrones were put in place,
> And the Ancient of Days was seated;
> His garment was white as snow,
> And the hair of His head was like pure wool.
> His throne was a fiery flame,
> Its wheels a burning fire;
> A fiery stream issued
> And came forth from before Him.
> A thousand thousands ministered to Him;
> Ten thousands times ten thousand stood before Him.

---

20 **Revelation 21:27** "But there shall by no means enter it anything that defiles, or causes an abomination or a lie, but only those who are written in the Lamb's Book of Life."
21 **Revelation 22:2** "And in the middle of its street, and on either side of the river, was the tree of life, which bore twelve fruits, each tree yielding its fruit every month. And the leaves of the tree were for the healing of the nations." See also Revelation 22:1, 19.
22 Daniel 7:9-10, 13-14.

> I was watching in the night visions,
> And behold, One like the Son of Man,
> Coming with the clouds of heaven!
> He came to the Ancient of Days,
> And they brought Him near before Him.
> Then to Him was given dominion and a glory and a kingdom,
> That all peoples, nations, and languages should serve Him.
> His dominion is an everlasting dominion,
> Which shall not pass away,
> And His kingdom the one
> Which shall not be destroyed.

I Believe . . .

The return of Jesus is the blessed hope that all Christians await. Every person will be raised from the dead to face judgment for their works, then be either granted eternal reward or sentenced to eternal punishment. God's kingdom will come fully, and God will reign eternally without a rival.

Questions for Study

1. What are some categories of topics in prophecy studies?
2. When people deny the future return of Christ, what kind of lifestyle do they tend to have?
3. What errors of lifestyle follow from the error of denying the resurrection?
4. At the judgment, people will be judged for their _____.

5. Those who deny the judgment seek to lower the significance of _____.

6. What is the final event revealed in God's schedule?

Recommended Reading

Culbertson, Paul T. & Wiley, H. Orton. *Introduction to Christian Theology*. Kansas City, MO: Beacon Hill Press, 1949. See Unit VII, "The Doctrine of Last Things."

Hitchcock, Mark. *A Complete Book of Bible Prophecy*. Wheaton, IL: Tyndale House, 1999.

20

The Ancient Creeds

During the first few centuries after Pentecost, the church found it necessary to clarify such concepts as the Trinity and the incarnation of Christ. They tried to discern if certain new ideas contradicted biblical truth. They established doctrinal standards as a defense against heresy. These standards were expressed in creeds, which were intended to be summaries of the fundamental truths that every Christian believed. Obviously the creeds could not cover every issue that would ever arise, but a person would scarcely have been considered a Christian if he denied anything in those early creeds, because they were attempts to concisely define the Christian faith.

Here are four of the early creeds of the church.

The Apostles' Creed

The Apostles' Creed was not written by the apostles, but it was written in the second century with the purpose of expressing the doctrines of the apostles.

> I believe in God the Father Almighty, Maker of heaven and earth;
>
> And in Jesus Christ, His only Son our Lord; who was conceived by the Holy Ghost, born of the Virgin Mary; suffered under Pontius Pilate; was crucified, dead and buried; He descended into hell; the third day He rose again from the dead; He ascended into heaven, and sits on the right

hand of God the Father Almighty; from thence He shall come to judge the quick and dead.

I believe in the Holy Ghost; the Holy Catholic Church; the communion of the saints; the forgiveness of sins; the resurrection of the body; and the life everlasting. Amen.

It seems that this creed was intended to expose the errors of those who denied that Jesus was truly human and virgin born. There were also some who denied that Jesus truly died, or that He physically rose from the dead. There were some religions, like many today, that denied that the world is moving toward a final judgment.

Very little is said about the Holy Spirit. That is not because the church did not know Who the Holy Spirit is; it is because heresies about His identity were not yet challenging the church. The term Catholic Church simply means "universal" and means that there is one true Christianity. "Forgiveness of sins" implies salvation by grace rather than by works or ritual. The resurrection of the body contrasted with the erroneous idea that all matter is evil by nature.

The Nicene Creed

The Nicene Creed was established at a church council in 325 to deal with heresies that denied the deity of Christ and the Holy Spirit. A few statements were added in 381. Notice that this creed does not contradict anything said in the Apostle's Creed, but it deals with issues that had not arisen previously.

I believe in one God, the Father Almighty, Maker of heaven and earth, and of all things visible and invisible.

And in one Lord Jesus Christ, the only begotten Son of God; begotten of His Father before all worlds, God of God, Light of light, Very God of very God, begotten, not made; being of one substance with the Father; by whom all things were made;

who for us men and for our salvation came down from heaven, and was incarnate by the Holy Ghost of the Virgin Mary, and was made man; and was crucified also for us under Pontius Pilate; He suffered and was buried; and the third day He arose again according to the scriptures; and ascended into heaven; and sits on the right hand of the Father; and He shall come again, with glory, to judge both the quick and the dead: whose kingdom shall have no end.

And I believe in the Holy Ghost, the Lord and Giver of Life, who proceeds from the Father and the Son; who with the Father and Son together is worshiped and glorified; who spake by the prophets;

And I believe in one Catholic and Apostolic Church; I acknowledge one baptism for the remission of sins; and I look for the resurrection of the dead; and the life of the world to come. Amen.

Here we see the statements expanded about all three persons of the Trinity. The full deity of Christ is emphasized in a way to safeguard it against those who would claim to believe that Jesus was God, yet minimize His deity. He is eternal ("before all worlds"), not created, and consists of whatever the Father consists of. Jesus is to be called God for the same reasons that the Father is to be called God.

"Apostolic" means the original church established through the doctrine and ministry of the apostles. Anyone who claimed to be a Christian but denied the doctrines of the apostles would be considered part of a new religion and not a Christian.

The Chalcedonian Creed

The Chalcedonian Creed was written in 451 to further protect the essential doctrines of the incarnation. The wording is not all easy to understand, but the concern of the writers was to protect the doctrines of the full deity and full humanity of Christ, without either aspect being so minimized as to become meaningless. Notice that at the end the writers stated that they considered these doctrines to be both scriptural and traditional in the church. They did not consider themselves to be developing new ideas, but only defending what the church had always believed.

> We, then, following the holy Fathers, all with one consent, teach men to confess one and the same Son, our Lord Jesus Christ, the same perfect in Godhead and also perfect in Manhood; truly God and truly man, of a reasonable soul and body; consubstantial with the Father according to the Godhead, and consubstantial with us according to the Manhood; in all things like unto us, without sin; begotten before all ages of the Father according to the Godhead, and in these latter days, for us and for our salvation, born of the Virgin Mary, the mother of God, according to the Manhood; one and the same Christ, Son, Lord, only begotten, to be acknowledged in two natures, inconfusedly, unchangeably, indivisibly, inseparably; the distinction of natures by no means being taken away by the union, but rather the properties of each nature being preserved, and concurring in one Person and one Subsistence, not parted or divided into two persons, but one and the same Son, and only begotten, God the Word, the Lord Jesus Christ; as the prophets from the beginning concerning him, and the Lord Jesus Christ himself has taught us, and the Creed of the holy Fathers has handed down to us.

The deity of Christ that early Christians affirmed was not some theoretical deity that Jesus had in heaven but not on earth. They believed that He was a true incarnation, God in the flesh. He possessed completely the attributes of God and man together while on earth. They considered this nature of Christ to be His indispensable qualification as Saviour.

The Athanasian Creed

The Athanasian Creed has been attributed to Athanasius, a bishop in the fourth century who exerted great influence yet suffered much persecution in his stand for the Trinity and for the deity of Christ.

Whosoever will be saved, before all things it is necessary that he hold the Catholic Faith. Which Faith except everyone do keep whole and undefiled, without doubt he shall perish everlastingly.

And the Catholic Faith is this:
That we worship one God in Trinity, and Trinity in Unity, neither confounding the Persons, nor dividing the Substance. For there is one Person of the Father, another of the Son, and another of the Holy Ghost. But the Godhead of the Father, of the Son, and of the Holy Ghost, is all one, the Glory equal, the Majesty co-eternal. Such as the Father is, such is the Son, and such is the Holy Ghost.

The Father uncreated, the Son uncreated, and the Holy Ghost uncreated. The Father incomprehensible, the Son incomprehensible, and the Holy Ghost incomprehensible. The Father eternal, the Son eternal, and the Holy Ghost eternal.

And yet they are not three eternals, but one eternal. As also there are not three incomprehensibles, nor three uncreated, but one uncreated, and one incomprehensible.

So likewise the Father is Almighty, the Son Almighty, and the Holy Ghost Almighty. And yet they are not three Almighties, but one Almighty. So the Father is God, the Son is God, and the Holy Ghost is God. And yet they are not three Gods, but one God. So likewise the Father is Lord, the Son Lord, and the Holy Ghost Lord. And yet not three Lords, but one Lord.

For like as we are compelled by the Christian verity to acknowledge every Person by himself to be both God and

Lord, So are we forbidden by the Catholic Religion to say, There be three Gods, or three Lords. The Father is made of none, neither created, nor begotten. The Son is of the Father alone, not made, nor created, but begotten. The Holy Ghost is of the Father and of the Son, neither made, nor created, nor begotten, but proceeding.

So there is one Father, not three Fathers; one Son, not three Sons; one Holy Ghost, not three Holy Ghosts. And in this Trinity none is afore, or after other; none is greater, or less than another; But the whole three Persons are co-eternal together and co-equal. So that in all things, as is aforesaid, the Unity in Trinity and the Trinity in Unity is to be worshipped. He therefore that will be saved must think thus of the Trinity.

Furthermore, it is necessary to everlasting salvation that he also believe rightly the Incarnation of our Lord Jesus Christ. For the right Faith is, that we believe and confess, that our Lord Jesus Christ, the Son of God, is God and Man; God, of the substance of the Father, begotten before the worlds; and Man of the substance of his Mother, born in the world; Perfect God and perfect Man, of a reasonable soul and human flesh subsisting.

Equal to the Father, as touching his Godhead; and inferior to the Father, as touching his manhood; Who, although he be God and Man, yet he is not two, but one Christ; One, not by conversion of the Godhead into flesh but by taking of the Manhood into God; One altogether; not by confusion of Substance, but by unity of Person. For as the reasonable soul and flesh is one man, so God and Man is one Christ; Who suffered for our salvation, descended into hell, rose again the third day from the dead. He ascended into heaven, he sits at the right hand of the Father, God Almighty, from whence he will come to judge the quick and the dead. At whose coming all men will rise again with their bodies and shall give account for their own works. And they that have done good shall go into life everlasting; and they that have done evil into everlasting fire.

This is the Catholic Faith, which except a man believe faithfully, he cannot be saved.

In the first few centuries there were not denominations as we have today. There was one church. So the creeds were statements made by the consensus of Christianity. Even today, most denominations that claim to honor the authority of the Bible hold the points of the creeds, though they may disagree on many other ideas.

Most Christian institutions today write summaries of their beliefs that are similar to the ancient creeds. In the box below is a short creed written by the faculty of God's Bible School and College, called the "Chapel Creed." A creed like the one below is not intended to replace the early creeds or to share their status, but to emphasize some of the most important truths in familiar terms.

I Believe . . .

I believe in God the Father, Creator of all things. And in Jesus Christ, His only Son, our Lord; who was conceived by the Holy Spirit, born of the Virgin Mary, suffered for us, and was crucified, dead and buried. He descended into hell; and, on the third day He arose again. He ascended into Heaven where He is seated at the right hand of God the Father Almighty. He will come again to judge the living and the dead. I believe in the Holy Spirit, who inspired the Holy Scriptures; who by grace justifies us through faith alone; and, who also sanctifies us into the likeness of Jesus Christ. I believe in the Holy Christian Church, the means of grace, the resurrection of the body, and life everlasting. Amen

Questions for Study

1. What was the purpose of the creeds?
2. What erroneous ideas about Jesus did the Apostles' Creed correct?
3. What does the term **catholic** mean in the creeds?
4. On what issues does the Nicene Creed focus most?
5. To what does the term **apostolic** refer in the Nicene Creed?
6. What doctrines were protected by the Chalcedonian Creed?

Recommended Reading

Bettenson, Henry, ed. *Documents of the Christian Church*. New York: Oxford University Press, 1967.

Noll, Mark A. *Turning Points*. Grand Rapids: Baker, 1997.

Appendix

Answers to Questions for Study

Chapter 1: God's Book

1. What can be understood about God from observation of creation.
2. In the inspiration of the Bible and the incarnation of Jesus Christ.
3. It describes God, explains the Fall and sin, and shows the way to be reconciled to God.
4. That it is the Word of God.
5. Because it is inspired of God.
6. They were "carried along" by the Holy Spirit (2 Peter 1:21-22).
7. Audible voice, dreams, visions, giving understanding and superintendence.
8. It is the Word of God.
9. It cannot fail, can be trusted, and will never mislead us.
10. It is without error in every statement it makes.

Chapter 2: Who is God?

1. To be wrong about what God is like.
2. That He is the Creator of all (and by implication, He is distinct from all).
3. Attributes
4. In order as follows:
    A. Spirit
    B. Eternal

- C. Personal
- D. Unchanging
- E. All-powerful
- F. Present everywhere
- G. Love
- H. Trinity
- I. Holiness
- J. Righteous
- K. Knows everything

Chapter 3: The Trinity

1. In the threefold design of the universe: space, time, and matter, each consisting in three aspects.
2. There is only one God; the Father, Son, and Holy Spirit are all God; and the three of them relate to each other as distinct persons.
3. The Son has always been the Son of the Father, and the Holy Spirit proceeds from the Father.
4. The family and the church.
5. We are to live in loving, self-giving relationships, emphasizing community.
6. We recognize that each person of the Trinity deserves worship. We pray to the Father, through the Son, in the Spirit, but we also pray to all persons of the Trinity.

Chapter 4: To Be Human

1. That we have a special purpose, that our life has a design, and we are accountable.
2. The moral instinct, free will, creative instinct, capacity to think and reason, capacity for relationship, self awareness, immortality, and capacity to worship.
3. To understand the concepts of right and wrong.
4. We can see the ethical and practical issues. We can carefully make life-altering decisions.

5. The ability to think about thinking itself, to consider whether certain thinking is really logical.
6. They have the innate capacities of humanity.
7. Man does not have free will except by grace. Sinful man uses his abilities in ways that are opposed to God.

Chapter 5: Sin—The Root of Every Problem

1. The root of every problem in the world is sin.
2. The word sin means "to miss the mark."
3. Scripture uses the word sin to refer to
   a) any action, attitude, or desire that misses the mark of God's law.
   b) the corrupt self-centeredness we are all born with that causes us to miss the mark of God's law.
4. The primary terms the Bible uses for the principle of sin are "sin," "the law of sin," and "the flesh."
5. The principle of sin or law of sin is the corruption of man's inner spiritual nature that resulted when Adam forfeited his sanctifying, life-giving relationship with God.
6. Depravity is the corruption of our inner nature that makes us self-centered and naturally inclined to commit sin.
7. Total depravity means that our whole being, not just part of us, has been corrupted.
8. Romans 13:10-18.
9. In addition to sinning with our actions, we can sin in our attitudes and our desires.
10. One of the primary reasons God put Leviticus in the Bible is to teach sinful people what sin is and how to have it forgiven so that they could be holy and live in fellowship with a holy God.
11. The three crucial truths that Leviticus teaches us about acts of sin are:
    a) God is serious about sin.
    b) There must be a blood sacrifice for sin to be forgiven.
    c) God views different kinds of sin differently.

12. Leviticus distinguishes two kinds of sinful acts: unintentional acts and intentional acts.
13. Unintentional sin is a violation of God's word when you did not intend to do wrong or you didn't realize you were doing something that was wrong.
14. Intentional sin is deliberately doing what you know is wrong.
15. The primary way we know that human infirmities are not sin is Hebrew 4:15 tells us that Jesus was without sin, and three verses later (5:2) the Hebrew writer says that Jesus was "compassed with infirmity."
16. The five major stages in which the plan of salvation unfolds are:
    a) initial salvation (i.e., when we are saved)
    b) entire sanctification
    c) progressive sanctification
    d) glorification
    e) resurrection to immortality
17. The five reasons that unintentional violations of God's word are called sins are:
    a) God calls them sin.
    b) They are offenses against God's holiness.
    c) They required the sacrifice of Jesus' life on the cross to propitiate God's wrath against us and remove our guilt.
    d) God requires us to repent and make restitution for these unintentional violations of His word.
    e) They will reap us corruption.
18. He should ask forgiveness and purpose by God's grace to avoid making that error again.
19. 1 Corinthians 10:13 "No temptation has overtaken you except such as is common to man; but God is faithful, who will not allow you to be tempted beyond what you are able, but with the temptation will also make the way of escape, that you may be able to bear it."

Chapter 6: Knowing Jesus

1. He is both God and man.
2. He was able to suffer and die; He represented us in His righteous life and sacrificial death; and He represents us as our high priest.
3. The answer should explain the significance of John 10:30 and 8:58, or discuss verses mentioned under the points "He Performed Divine Acts..." and "He is Creator and Sustainer."
4. His sacrifice was of infinite value; He has the power to save us; and He is to be worshipped.
5. As a sacrifice, providing the basis of our forgiveness.
6. It proved His victory over sin and death; it proved His identity (thus proving the gospel); it shows that He will be able to raise us from the dead.

Chapter 7: The Holy Spirit

1. He has a mind, a will, and emotions.
2. The answer should explain the significance of some of the following: Acts 5:3-4, 2 Timothy 3:16, 1 Corinthians 6:19, and John 3:5-8.
3. So that we give Him the respect and honor He deserves.
4. He convicts of sin, regenerates, sanctifies, gives assurance, empowers, and gives understanding of the Bible. Other activities are listed in the chapter.
5. All three.
6. When he is saved.
7. Surrender to God completely, and ask in faith.

Chapter 8: Satan—Our Chief Enemy

1. Satan was created to be an archangel.
2. He is a spirit.
3. Because he hates God, in whose image man is made.

4. Only perverted forms of pleasures that God created.
5. The lake of fire.
6. They think they are gaining power for personal use.
7. More people would turn to God because of fear of Satan.

Chapter 9: Salvation—God's Provision

1. Before the foundation of the world (Eph. 1:4).
2. We are all sinful by nature and by choice; we are slaves to sin; we are God's enemies and alienated from Him; our understanding is darkened, and our hearts are blinded; we are dying physically; we have already been judged and sentenced to separation from God in the Lake of Fire.
3. The Old Testament sacrificial system teaches us that:
   a) God is both just and merciful.
   b) Salvation required a perfect sacrifice and the shedding of blood.
   c) Salvation involved a substitutionary sacrifice.
   d) Salvation required a divine sacrifice.
4. Jesus' death on the cross demonstrates God's justice in that the penalty for our sin was paid. Jesus' death on the cross demonstrates God's mercy in that He provided a means for us to be forgiven and made it freely available to all.
5. Jesus had to shed his blood because God requires blood to be shed for sin to be atoned (Heb. 9:22).
6. The word atonement means "at-one-ness" Theologians use this word because one of God's purposes in the atonement is to bring fallen mankind back into the unity of a relationship with Him.
7. The primary purpose of the atonement was to deal with the problem of our sin so that we could be reconciled to God and live in holy, loving fellowship with Him for eternity.
8. Being reconciled to God means that our broken relationship with God has been restored. There is peace between us.

9. God is propitiated when His righteous wrath against sin and His righteous justice are satisfied by the sacrifice of His Son.
10. We are redeemed in the sense that we were formerly slaves to sin, but God has bought us back through the blood of Jesus.
11. 1 John 2:2 teaches that Jesus died for the sins of the whole world and not only for the sins of Christians.
12. Titus 2:11.

Chapter 10: Salvation—God's Work and Our Response

1. Prevenient grace.
2. Grace is anything God gives us that we do not deserve. Prevenient grace is the grace that God gives us before we are saved that enables us to respond to the light (truth) He gives us.
3. Titus 2:11 says, "For the grace of God that brings salvation has appeared to all men."
4. John 6:44 says that no one can come to the Father unless He draws him. Unless the Father draws us, we can't come.
5. The Holy Spirit convicts our consciences of guilt, makes us aware of God's justice, and shows us the penalty for sin.
6. Repentance and faith.
7. Repentance is a change of mind and heart about sin that results in a change of behavior. When we repent, we stop sinning and start doing what we know is right.
8. Faith is believing what God has said, committing to do what He requires, and trusting in and resting on His promises.
9. No, meeting the conditions for salvation does not earn us salvation nor does it mean that we deserve to be saved. Romans 4:4-5 makes it clear that God does not owe us anything. Salvation is His free gift to us.
10. First we must believe that Jesus is the Son of God, that his sacrifice on the cross was sufficient for our sins, and that He rose bodily from the grave. Second, we must leave our sins

and begin serving God. Third, we must believe that He does forgive us when we have met His requirements for salvation.

11. The logical order is: God unites us with Christ, justifies us, sanctifies (regenerates) us, adopts us, and seals us with the Holy Spirit.

12. (1) He forgives our sins. (2) He blots out the record of our sins. (3) He credits our faith as righteousness. (4) He declares us to be righteous. (5) He accepts us for Christ's sake.

13. Our justification is based on our union with Christ.

14. God sets us apart from our old life of sin, claims us as His own, makes us holy, and begins transforming us into the likeness of Christ.

15. Regeneration is a term that means "rebirth." Regeneration is part of initial sanctification.

16. When we are born again, we become part of God's family. When God adopts us, He grants us all the rights and privileges that come with being His children.

17. When God "seals" us with the Holy Spirit, He places the Holy Spirit in us as the sign that we are genuinely His children and as a guarantee of the future inheritance we will receive.

Chapter 11: An Introduction to Christian Holiness

1. The will of God for us.
2. Because God gives the command to humans, and provides the needed grace.
3. When he is saved.
4. Separation as God's special possession, separation from all that is ordinary (not dedicated to God), and separation from all sin.
5. See the list at the end of the chapter.

Chapter 12: Understanding Entire Sanctification

1. 1 Thessalonians 5:23.

2. Initial sanctification, progressive sanctification, and entire sanctification.

3. Initial sanctification refers to the work of God through the Holy Spirit at the moment we are born again by which He sets us apart to Himself as His possession, separates us from the practice of willful sin, and begins the process of making us like Jesus Christ.

4. Progressive sanctification refers to the on-going work of the Holy Spirit daily transforming us into the likeness of Christ. Progressive sanctification begins at the moment of conversion and continues throughout life until glorification in heaven.

5. Entire sanctification refers to a specific further working of God in the heart and life of a Christian by which God cleanses his heart from self-centeredness (inherited depravity), and fills him with the Holy Spirit, thereby enabling him to love God completely—with all his heart, mind, soul, and strength (with no rivals, reservations, or self-centered motives)—and his neighbor as himself. Entire sanctification also empowers the Christian to serve Christ more effectively.

6. It is God's will. God wishes to remove the remaining self-centeredness from our life.

7. In entire sanctification our relationship with God is strengthened.

Chapter 13: Steps to Entire Sanctification

1. By becoming aware of his self-centeredness and by believing the testimony of Scripture that it is God's desire for every Christian to be entirely sanctified.

2. Paul explains when he uses the adverb entirely, that he is speaking of a work of God's sanctifying grace that purifies every part of man: "spirit, soul, and body."

3. These questions are to deepen personal understanding and assist personal application.

Chapter 14: The Three Pillars of Assurance

1. That we are saved and entirely sanctified.
2. The assurance of faith in God's word.
3. To believe what God says, to commit to do what God requires, and to trust in and to rest on what God promises.
4. The witness of the Spirit.
5. Because it is not strong or clear at all times.
6. Through measurable attitudes and actions, we can examine ourselves to see if we are truly in the faith.

Chapter 15: The Church—The Home Where We Belong

1. The church is the family of God, of which every believer is a member.
2. "The gates of hell shall not prevail against it."
3. Baptism is a public confession of faith in Christ, and the Lord's Supper is a reminder of His death for us.
4. Believers serve one another by use of spiritual gifts.
5. Because the intention of the church is to draw in sinners and redeem them.
6. The church is one, holy, universal, and apostolic.
7. The church is to a temple of praise, a witness and guardian of the gospel, a teacher of the faithful, an agent for moral reform, and an evangelistic agency.

Chapter 16: Christ's Triumphant Return

1. Jesus' coming will be visible to the whole world.
2. Anything opposed to God will be defeated.
3. Christians will be honored and rewarded. They will rise to meet Him. They will rule with Him.
4. They will be resurrected at the time of His coming.

5. We must stay on guard spiritually so that we are not unprepared when the Lord returns.
6. It will be like lightning and like the twinkling of an eye.
7. A list of four considerations is given. A reason for the long time is that people are given time to repent.
8. The world will be changed suddenly.
9. We should live in spiritual victory, with eternal values, and focused on the mission of reaching the lost.

Chapter 17: Heaven—Eternal Life With God

1. We are flesh and blood, while God (whose home heaven is) is Spirit. God is infinite. Heaven does not have the earthly limitations of time and space.
2. Since God has the power to make heaven exactly what He wants, it is consistent with His nature.
3. Pain, sorrow, conflicts, danger, sickness, aging, and death. All results of the curse.
4. Walls of jasper, gates of pearl, foundations of rare gems, and streets of gold.
5. Those who are saved. See fuller answer in the chapter.
6. At death or at the return of Jesus, whichever comes first.
7. We know that what God created for earth will be exceeded by what He has created for heaven.

Chapter 18: Eternal Punishment

1. It would be better to cut off any action that we are doing than to go to hell for it.
2. Answers may vary, but from the text, "Hell is eternal, irrevocable, and agonizing."
3. Atheists, Jehovah's Witnesses, Mormons, and Universalists.
4. Because sin is an offense against an infinite God, because the sinner denies God the eternal worship and service owed, and

because we are eternal beings with no other place to go if we choose separation from God.

5. By repentance and faith in Jesus Christ.

6. Discussion question: Answers may vary, but see the paragraph beginning with the words, "Some refuse to believe in hell because they wonder . . . ."

Chapter 19: Final Events

1. Speculative issues, controversies among evangelicals, and necessary truths.

2. They live for earthly priorities. They emphasize what man can do instead of what God can and will do.

3. Devaluing the body can lead to either an indulgence of physical desires or an extreme suppression of them.

4. Works.

5. Human choices.

6. The coming of God's complete and eternal kingdom, beginning eternity.

Chapter 20: The Ancient Creeds

1. To summarize the truths every Christian believed, or, to define the Christian faith.

2. That he was not fully human, not virgin born, did not truly die, or did not rise from the dead.

3. "Universal," emphasizing that there is only one church—one Christianity.

4. The deity of Jesus and the Holy Spirit.

5. The original church established through the doctrine and ministry of the apostles.

6. Doctrines of the incarnation—the full deity and humanity of Jesus.